The
Cuban
Americans

THE IMMIGRANT EXPERIENCE

The Cuban Americans

Renée Gernand

Sandra Stotsky, General Editor
Harvard University Graduate School of Education

CHELSEA HOUSE PUBLISHERS

New York • Philadelphia

CHELSEA HOUSE PUBLISHERS

Editorial Director: Richard Rennert
Executive Managing Editor: Karyn Gullen Browne
Copy Chief: Robin James
Picture Editor: Adrian G. Allen
Art Director: Robert Mitchell
Manufacturing Director: Gerald Levine
Assistant Art Director: Joan Ferrigno

THE IMMIGRANT EXPERIENCE

Editors: Rebecca Stefoff and Reed Ueda

Staff for THE CUBAN AMERICANS

Assistant Editor: Annie McDonnell
Copy Editor: Apple Kover
Designer: Lydia Rivera
Cover Illustrator: Jane Sterrett

3 5 7 9 8 6 4 2

Library of Congress Cataloging-in-Publication Data

Gernand, Renèe.
  The Cuban Americans / Renèe Gernand.
  p. cm.—(The immigrant experience)
  Includes bibliographical references and index.
  ISBN 0-7910-3354-6.
      0-7910-3376-7 (pbk.)
  1. Cuban Americans—Juvenile literature. [1. Cuban Americans.] I. Title. II. Series.
E184.C97G47   1996   94-42011
973'.0468729—dc20   CIP
                                                                AC

CONTENTS

THE IMMIGRANT EXPERIENCE

CHELSEA HOUSE PUBLISHERS

A
NATION OF
NATIONS

Daniel Patrick Moynihan

The Constitution of the United States begins: "We the People of the United States…" Yet, as we know, the United States is not made up of a single group of people. It is made up of many peoples. Immigrants from Europe, Asia, Africa, and Central and South America settled in North America seeking a new life filled with opportunities unavailable in their homeland. Coming from many nations, they forged one nation and made it their own. More than 100 years ago, Walt Whitman expressed this perception of America as a melting pot: "Here is not merely a nation, but a teeming Nation of nations."

Although the ingenuity and acts of courage of these immigrants, our ancestors, shaped the North American way of life, we sometimes take their contributions for granted. This fine series, *The Immigrant Experience*, examines the experiences and contributions of the immigrants and how these contributions determined the future of the United States and Canada.

Immigrants did not abandon their ethnic traditions when they reached the shores of North America. Each ethnic group had its own customs and traditions, and each brought different experiences, accomplishments, skills, values, styles of dress, and tastes in food that lingered long after its arrival. Yet this profusion of differences created a singularity, or bond, among the immigrants.

The United States and Canada are unusual in this respect. Whereas religious and ethnic differences have sparked intolerance throughout the rest of the world—from the 17th-century religious wars to the 19th-century nationalist movements in Europe to the near extermination of the Jewish people under Nazi Germany—North Americans have struggled to learn how to respect each other's differences and live in harmony.

Millions of immigrants from scores of homelands brought diversity to our continent. In a mass migration, some 12 million immigrants passed through the waiting rooms of New York's Ellis Island; thousands more came to the West Coast. At first, these immigrants were welcomed because labor was needed to meet the demands of the Industrial Age. Soon, however, the new immigrants faced the prejudice of earlier immigrants who saw them as a burden on the economy. Legislation was passed to limit immigration. The Chinese Exclusion Act of 1882 was among the first laws closing the doors to the promise of America. The Japanese were also effectively excluded by this law. In 1924, Congress set immigration quotas on a country-by-country basis.

Such prejudices might have triggered war, as they did in Europe, but North Americans chose negotiation and compromise, instead. This determination to resolve differences peacefully has been the hallmark of the peoples of North America.

The remarkable ability of Americans to live together as one people was seriously threatened by the issue of slavery. It was a symptom of growing intolerance in the world. Thousands of settlers from the British Isles had arrived in the colonies as indentured servants, agreeing to work for a specified number of years on farms or as apprentices in return for passage to America and room and board. When the first Africans arrived in the then-British colonies during the 17th century, some colonists thought that they too should be treated as indentured servants. Eventually, the question of whether the Africans should be viewed as indentured, like the English, or as slaves who could be owned for life, was considered in a Maryland court. The court's calamitous decree held that blacks were slaves bound to lifelong servitude, and so were their children.

America went through a time of moral examination and civil war before it finally freed African slaves and their descendants. The principle that all people are created equal had faced its greatest challenge and survived.

Yet the court ruling that set blacks apart from other races fanned flames of discrimination that burned long after slavery was abolished—and that still flicker today. The concept of racism had existed for centuries in countries throughout the world. For instance, when the Manchus conquered China in the 17th century, they decreed that Chinese and Manchus could not intermarry. To impress their superiority on the conquered Chinese, the Manchus ordered all Chinese men to wear their hair in a long braid called a queue.

By the 19th century, some intellectuals took up the banner of racism, citing Charles Darwin. Darwin's scientific studies hypothesized that highly evolved animals were dominant over other animals. Some advocates of this theory applied it to humans, asserting that certain races were more highly evolved than others and thus were superior.

This philosophy served as the basis for a new form of discrimination, not only against nonwhite people but also against various ethnic groups. Asians faced harsh discrimination and were depicted by popular 19th-century newspaper cartoonists as depraved, degenerate, and deficient in intelligence. When the Irish flooded American cities to escape the famine in Ireland, the cartoonists caricatured the typical "Paddy" (a common term for Irish immigrants) as an apelike creature with jutting jaw and sloping forehead.

By the 20th century, racism and ethnic prejudice had given rise to virulent theories of a Northern European master race. When Adolf Hitler came to power in Germany in 1933, he popularized the notion of Aryan supremacy. "Aryan," a term referring to the Indo-European races, was applied to so-called superior physical characteristics such as blond hair, blue eyes, and delicate facial features. Anyone with darker and heavier features was considered inferior. Buttressed by these theories, the German Nazi state from

1933 to 1945 set out to destroy European Jews, along with Poles, Russians, and other groups considered inferior. It nearly succeeded. Millions of these people were exterminated.

The tragedies brought on by ethnic and racial intolerance throughout the world demonstrate the importance of North America's efforts to create a society free of prejudice and inequality.

A relatively recent example of the New World's desire to resolve ethnic friction nonviolently is the solution the Canadians found to a conflict between two ethnic groups. A long-standing dispute as to whether Canadian culture was properly English or French resurfaced in the mid-1960s, dividing the peoples of the French-speaking Quebec Province from those of the English-speaking provinces. Relations grew tense, then bitter, then violent. The Royal Commission on Bilingualism and Biculturalism was established to study the growing crisis and to propose measures to ease the tensions. As a result of the commission's recommendations, all official documents and statements from the national government's capital at Ottawa are now issued in both French and English, and bilingual education is encouraged.

The year 1980 marked a coming of age for the United States's ethnic heritage. For the first time, the U.S. Census asked people about their ethnic background. Americans chose from more than 100 groups, including French Basque, Spanish Basque, French Canadian, Afro-American, Peruvian, Armenian, Chinese, and Japanese. The ethnic group with the largest response was English (49.6 million). More than 100 million Americans claimed ancestors from the British Isles, which includes England, Ireland, Wales, and Scotland. There were almost as many Germans (49.2 million) as English. The Irish-American population (40.2 million) was third, but the next largest ethnic group, the Afro-Americans, was a distant fourth (21 million). There was a sizable group of French ancestry (13 million), as well as of Italian (12 million). Poles, Dutch, Swedes, Norwegians, and Russians followed. These groups, and other smaller ones, represent the wondrous profusion of ethnic influences in North America.

Canada, too, has learned more about the diversity of its population. Studies conducted during the French/English conflict showed that Canadians were descended from Ukrainians, Germans, Italians, Chinese, Japanese, native Indians, and Eskimos, among others. Canada found it had no ethnic majority, although nearly half of its immigrant population had come from the British Isles. Canada, like the United States, is a land of immigrants for whom mutual tolerance is a matter of reason as well as principle.

The people of North America are the descendants of one of the greatest migrations in history. And that migration is not over. Koreans, Vietnamese, Nicaraguans, Cubans, and many others are heading for the shores of North America in large numbers. This mix of cultures shapes every aspect of our lives. To understand ourselves, we must know something about our diverse ethnic ancestry. Nothing so defines the North American nations as the motto on the Great Seal of the United States: *E Pluribus Unum*—Out of Many, One. ⬥

Cuban Americans in Union City, New Jersey, celebrate their heritage in an annual parade.

A
PEOPLE
IN EXILE

A majority of the nearly 1 million Cuban Americans now living in the United States first entered the country as political refugees during the early 1960s. Unlike other ethnic groups—who saw America as a land of opportunity—Cuban exiles regarded the United States only as a temporary haven from the Communist regime that had taken over their native land in 1959. Most Cubans saw this radical swing toward communism as the latest chapter in a long and tumultuous national history. For nearly 400 years— from the early 1500s to 1898—Cuba had been a colony of Spain and had suffered under the yoke of that country's imperial policies. Yet, despite its exploitation by the Spanish, Cuba flourished and by the 19th century had become the largest sugar-producing nation in the world.

But prosperity alone did not satisfy the Cubans. They longed to liberate themselves from Spanish rule and succeeded in doing so with the help of the United States, which in 1898 defeated Spain in a conflict now known as the Spanish-American War. Cuba finally won independence, but its autonomy proved short-lived. The American government soon made clear that it intended to control Cuba, and U.S. businesses dominated the country's economy and political life.

In the early 1960s thousands of Cubans migrated to America to escape the regime of Fidel Castro.

During the next 50 years Cubans grew to resent the interference of the United States in their country's domestic affairs. In particular, they objected to a series of corrupt, U.S.-backed presidents who obstructed the development of democracy within Cuba and terrorized the populace with a ruthless police force. One such leader, Fulgencio Batista, held Cuba in his sway for approximately 20 years until his reign was ended by a broad-based revolution in 1959, a rebellion led by a radical lawyer named Fidel Castro.

Castro soon proved as tyrannical as Batista had been. The "reforms" he implemented included a disastrous industrialization program that resulted in nationwide food shortages. By 1961 his popularity had waned so drastically that he formed an alliance with the Soviet Union in order to remain in power. During the same year he publicly proclaimed, "I am a Marxist-Leninist and will be one until the day I die," a pronouncement that sent Cuba's large middle class into a panic.

Victims of Castro's regime escaped Cuba any way they could. Most headed for the safety of the United States, 90 miles away, across the Straits of Florida. The majority of these early refugees were professionals who were allowed to take with them only five dollars in American currency and the clothing on their back. Men and women who had once managed government agencies, presided over courts of law, or practiced medicine suddenly found themselves reduced to poverty in the United States. For the first time in their lives they were forced to accept charity or to toil in menial jobs.

Many of these immigrants put down roots right where they landed, in the city of Miami—located only 150 miles from Cuba. Others participated in federally funded relocation programs that sent them into nearly every state in the Union, but the majority who left Florida preferred to settle elsewhere on the East Coast, in such urban centers as Washington, D.C., New York City, and in the townships of Hudson County, New Jersey, where nearly 47,000 Cuban Americans had made their home by 1980.

Although Cubans branched out across America, many still considered Miami their spiritual home. There they established the neighborhood known as "Little Havana" (named after Cuba's capital city), a district where residents could go from bank to grocery store to post office doing business in their native tongue, Spanish. Within a decade of their arrival, the Cubans' power extended beyond the perimeters of this ethnic enclave and into the fields of politics, real estate, and finance. As the influence of Cuban Americans grew, so did their numbers. In 1957 about 50,000 Cubans resided in the United States, but within 20 years the community swelled to perhaps 680,000, and by 1987 that number accounted for most of the Cuban population of the Miami area alone.

Cuban Americans seemed not merely to inhabit but to take over Miami, once an economically depressed tourist resort. Throughout the 1970s Cuban Americans became an indispensable part of the city's rapid economic growth, helping transform Miami into a "gateway to Latin America." Cubans won acclaim for their role in Miami's renaissance, but they also earned a reputation as participants in a less savory industry, the illegal drug trade. Cocaine smugglers from South America and the Caribbean found Florida a convenient point of entry into the United States and often employed Cubans as "middlemen." Articles about the wealth and brutality of these drug lords dominated

Men pass an afternoon in "Domino Park," located in Miami's Cuban neighborhood, Little Havana.

American press coverage of Miami, inspiring the popular television show "Miami Vice" and damaging the reputation of the city's Cubans, whom the public associated with this underworld.

The Cuban-American community gained additional notoriety from a few highly visible extremists who often resorted to terrorism to advance the cause of a non-Communist Cuba. The vast majority of Cuban Americans, however, were neither drug traffickers nor zealots but respectable citizens who represented a broad spectrum of society. In the mid-1980s, 35 percent of working Cuban Americans in Miami held professional jobs; another 35 percent were employed as sales clerks, technical workers, or office workers; and 30 percent were blue-collar workers. In the 1980s, community leaders spoke admiringly of the 4,500 physicians and 500 lawyers of Cuban descent practicing in the Miami area and often pointed out that Cuban Americans owned almost 20,000 businesses in Dade County, where Miami is located. They took even more pride in the preservation of traditional values that strengthened individual families and the community as a whole, enabling Cuban-Americans to contribute richly to the country they now called home. ✍

*On January 3, 1959,
revolutionary Cuban troops
ride in a triumphal procession
through Havana.*

THE PEARL
OF THE
ANTILLES

Cuba marks the northernmost territory of the Greater Antilles, a chain of Caribbean islands including Puerto Rico, Jamaica, and Hispaniola (an island now shared by the nations of Haiti and the Dominican Republic). The group remained unknown to the Western world until 1492, when an Italian navigator chanced upon it while looking for a legendary trade route to the Far East. Christopher Columbus mistook the Antilles for islands marking the coast of India and thus named them the "Indies," a misnomer that stuck and in time was modified to "West Indies." Although he delighted in all his new finds, Columbus was particularly enthralled with Cuba and called it "the fairest island human eyes have yet beheld." He quickly relayed news of this paradise to his patrons, King Ferdinand V and Queen Isabella of Spain.

At that time, Spain had become preeminent among the European powers because of its exploration and conquest of the New World. The country's coffers burst with gold purloined from Mexico, Peru, and Chile—Spain's possessions in Central and South America. Ferdinand and Isabella hoped that the West Indies would also yield a supply of precious metals. In 1511 they sent representatives to colonize the Caribbean, staking their first claim in Cuba, the largest of all the islands.

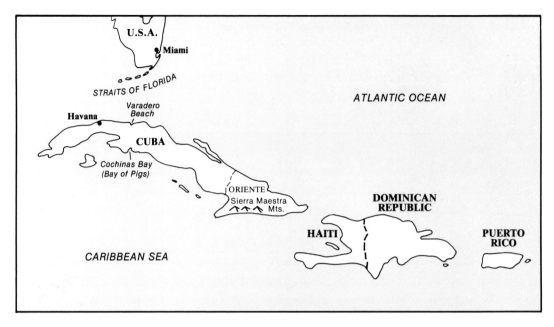

Early Colonial Cuba

By 1515 the Spaniard Diego Velázquez had founded at least seven settlements in Cuba. His project cost thousands of human lives, not those of the Spaniards, but those of the island's native population of Ciboney and Tainos Indians, two tribes in the Arawak federation. The peaceful Ciboney had traditionally made their living by fishing along Cuba's 2,175-mile coastline and by hunting farther inland in Cuba's abundant mountains and forests. Some Ciboney acted as servants to the more sophisticated Tainos, who had developed native agriculture and a primitive industry in pottery and textiles.

Unlike the powerful Aztec and Mayan Indians of Mexico and the mighty Incas of Peru, the Ciboney and Tainos of Cuba could muster no resistance to the Spanish, who easily conquered them with masterful horsemanship and sophisticated weaponry. By 1517, just six years after Velázquez first landed in Cuba, both groups had been wiped out by disease, suicide, and mistreatment at the hands of the Spanish. The few survivors included some Tainos leaders, chosen by colonists to manage their newly developed estates.

The annihilation of Cuba's indigenous population presented a problem for the Spanish, who had intended to cultivate sugarcane in the country's arable lowlands. Their plans to create a sugar industry were doomed unless they found workers to plant and harvest the crop, so the colonists decided to import slaves from Africa. In doing so, they changed the face of Cuban society. By the turn of the 19th century, blacks vastly outnumbered white colonists.

Cuba's slaves toiled long hours on the island's sugar plantations, yet they were never reduced to utter misery because they had opportunities to better their lot. Some blacks bought their liberty from owners and, once free, established their own small farms; some even became slave owners. In addition, the Spanish accorded mulattoes—as people of mixed race were called—many of the privileges, if not the status, of Spaniards. Still, the Spanish constituted an elite minority within Cuba and kept control of the island not with humane policies but with brute strength drawn from their vast supplies of guns and horses.

An engraving depicts Christopher Columbus and his crew landing in the New World.

The Colonial Prize

Although sporadic slave revolts sometimes seemed to weaken the colonists' hold on Cuba, the real threat to their continued control of the island was posed by seafaring European nations. Like Spain, these nations prowled the New World in search of territory they could claim as their own. In 1762, for example, British forces took over Cuba's capital, Havana, and held it for a year until they agreed to ransom it in exchange for the Spanish territory of Florida, just 90 miles northwest of Cuba's coast. Even when Havana itself was not under siege, the Spanish galleons anchored there often fell prey to French, British, and Dutch pirates who sought the bounty on board.

The perpetual danger of attack never deterred Spanish vessels from docking in Cuba's harbors. The island's proximity to both North and South America made it

A Caribbean tribe hunts rabbits and foxes in this engraving from 1624.

an ideal resting spot for treasure ships bound for the Spanish colonies of Mexico or Peru. But Cuba served as far more than a port for Spain, which dominated the economy of its colony, monitoring every peso that entered the country and every pound of sugar that left it. The Spanish crown regulated Cuba's main exports—sugar, and tobacco—and restricted the island from importing any goods except Spanish ones. Cuba's mother country also drained the colony's precious natural resources, including gold and silver, thus securing a ready supply of raw materials for Spanish industry. In the late 18th century, Cuba became an even more desirable possession when its sugar industry boomed. By 1793—when British forces invaded Cuba's competitor in the industry, Haiti—Cuba reigned as the region's undisputed king of sugar. Just four decades later, in the 1830s, Cuba became the largest sugar exporter in the world.

As Cubans kept a sharp eye on the rise and fall of the sugar trade in competing colonies, so, too, they watched the success or failure of the struggles for independence waged by other Spanish colonies in the western hemisphere. In Mexico, for example, a series of battles between 1810 and 1821 forced Spain to release this territory into the hands of Mexican settlers.

A political cartoon from 1868 depicts Secretary of State William Seward proposing the annexation of Cuba to Uncle Sam.

Most wealthy and powerful Cubans shied away from political agitation because they did not want to jeopardize trade with their largest partner, Spain. Domination by that nation—and even the corruption and incompetence of Spanish government officials on the island— seemed preferable to the financial ruin a colonial revolt might bring. The Cubans' longings for independence were, in the words of one expert, "drowned in a sea of sugar."

Even the most conservative colonists, however, could not ignore the recent success of the revolutionary war that the American colonies had waged against the British; nor could they help envying the democratic form of government that the revolutionaries had established. The Cubans' fascination with the United States equaled that of the new republic's with Cuba. Americans had been traveling to the island since the 1770s, when they were introduced there by Spain, a supporter during the colonies' war of independence.

As the 19th century dawned, the United States was expanding its frontiers. In 1803, President Thomas Jefferson negotiated the Louisiana Purchase, buying France's claim to 828,000 square miles of North American territory that now makes up all or part of 13 states between the Mississippi River and the Rocky Mountains. Jefferson also looked south. In 1809, he said, "We must have Cuba"—both because Cuba was an attractively prosperous territory and to dislodge Spain from its toehold so close to the United States.

In 1823, Secretary of State John Quincy Adams seconded Jefferson's opinion in a letter to the U.S. minister to Spain about the Caribbean islands:

These islands, from their local position, are natural appendages to the North American continent; and one of them, Cuba, almost in sight of our shores . . . has become an object of transcendent importance to the political and commercial interests of our Union . . . it is scarcely possible to resist conviction that the annexation

Colonial rebels unload a shipment of American arms during the Ten Years' War between Spain and Cuba.

of Cuba to our federal republic will be indispensable to the continuance and integrity of the Union itself.

Adams wanted to send a message to Spain and all other European powers that the Americas now fell within the influence of the United States. He persuaded President James Monroe to deliver this message in a speech to the U.S. Congress on December 2, 1823. One part of the speech, a warning to Europe to keep its distance from the Americas, has come to be called the Monroe Doctrine: "The American continents . . . are henceforth not to be considered as subjects for future colonization by any European powers." Over the years, Monroe's statement became the backbone of U.S. foreign policy in Latin America.

Adams never succeeded in winning Cuba for the United States, but he managed to convince Americans that the island was of vital importance to the national interest, and this belief influenced subsequent generations of politicians. In 1848, President James Polk offered Spain $100 million for Cuba, a proposal that irked the Spanish, who replied that they would rather see Cuba "sink into the ocean" than fall into American hands. Despite this rejection, the United States remained determined to annex the island. During the years before the Civil War, Southern states wooed Cuba in the hope of adding slave-owning territory to the republic and thus preventing free states from outnumbering them. Cuba again refused American advances.

The Ten Years' War

Most Cubans could not agree whether they wanted to be fully independent, to be an autonomous Spanish possession, or to be annexed to the United States. But all agreed that the Americans were a valuable ally. In 1868 the Cubans turned to the United States for military support when the island launched its first armed struggle against Spain. Known as the Ten Years' War, this conflict ended in defeat in 1878 and cost 250,000 Cuban lives. During the war, numerous Cuban separatists had foreseen a Spanish victory and fled the island. Many headed for the United States, where they were accepted as refugees.

The approximately 5,000 Cuban exiles who lived in the United States after the Ten Years' War watched impotently as Spain reclaimed their homeland. The mother country resumed its exploitation of the island, imposing backbreaking taxes, forbidding the Cubans to choose their own leadership, and quelling any attempted colonial uprisings. The Spanish abolished slavery in 1886, as they had promised, but they reneged on many other guarantees of reform. This betrayal incensed many Cuban patriots, none more so than José Martí, a revolutionary and writer who made his home in the United States from 1880 to 1895.

José Martí

The son of Spanish parents, Martí lived much of his life in exile from Cuba. In 1869 his revolutionary politics incurred the wrath of colonial authorities, who sentenced the 16-year-old Martí to six years in prison and afterward agreed to let him move to Spain, where he remained for four years studying law. In 1878, Martí returned to Cuba but again faced an enforced exile in Spain. Instead, he escaped to the United States in 1880. In New York, Martí won a reputation as a poet and journalist. His book of essays *Nuestra America* ("Our America"), published in 1891, examined Latin American culture and politics and earned him a wide following both in Cuba and abroad. Also during this period, he founded the Cuban Revolutionary Party and assumed its leadership in 1892.

In 1895 Martí returned home to help Cuba in its second fight for independence. The nation was again ripe for revolution after the price of sugar fell drastically from 8 cents per pound in 1884 to 2 cents in 1895, ruining the country's economy. Just after war broke out, Martí arrived to lead the island's rebels to victory but instead met his end in the Battle of Dos Ríos on May 19, 1895.

Cubans still regard José Martí as the greatest patriot in their history.

The Spanish-American War

Cuban field workers harvest sugar cane in about 1940.

For the next three years, Cubans battled the Spanish with some success, winning the full rights of Spanish citizenship and the chance to elect their own officials. But the Cubans would settle for nothing short of complete liberty, perhaps knowing that their ultimatum would be supported by their powerful ally to the north. The United States did not immediately jump into the fray between Cuba and Spain, but enthusiasm for the Cuban cause intensified in all sectors of American society. The popular press, particularly William Randolph Hearst's New York *Journal*, raised public sympathy for Cuba by publishing sensational stories of Spanish mistreatment of Cuban civilians.

By the beginning of 1898, the United States had developed a war fever that reached a hysterical pitch in February, when the U.S. battleship *Maine* was blown up by a Spanish submarine mine in Havana's harbor. Two hundred and sixty American soldiers were killed. President William McKinley, who once had urged that diplomacy, not force, be used to settle the conflict between Cuba and Spain, gave in to public pressure to declare war. In April 1898 he issued a resolution to Congress to send American troops to Cuba.

Although vastly outnumbered, the U.S. forces defeated Spain's troops within 10 weeks. Both Cuba and Puerto Rico, as well as Guam and the Philippines, emerged from the shadows of Spanish colonialism. But Cuba's independence was not complete. José Martí had once predicted that the "colossus of the North," the United States, would someday threaten Cuban independence, and in the years after the Spanish-American War that prediction came true. The U.S. Army had occupied Cuba during the war, but when the war ended the Americans remained on the island. The United States feared that one of two things would happen if it withdrew from Cuba: Spain would reassert its claim, or Cuba, whose people had no experience in self-government after centuries of colonial domination, would be engulfed in chaos.

The Platt Amendment

A constitutional convention met in Havana from November 1900 to February 1901 to draft a constitution. The United States pressured the convention into accepting the Platt Amendment, under which Cuba agreed to continue the sanitary measures that the U.S. Army had introduced to combat yellow fever and other diseases; to lease naval bases to the United States; and to permit U.S. military intervention if necessary to preserve order.

U.S. troops withdrew in 1902, and Tomas Estrada Palma took office as Cuba's first president. By this time, however, U.S. business interests owned or leased almost half of Cuba's farmland as well as a large share of its mines and other resources, and therefore the United States was concerned about political unrest or threats to economic stability in Cuba. On a number of occasions, Cuba erupted into violence: in 1906 there was an armed revolution against Palma's government, and in 1912 a

MAINE EXPLOSION CAUSED BY BOMB OR TORPEDO?

Capt. Sigsbee and Consul-General Lee Are in Doubt---The World Has Sent a Special Tug, With Submarine Divers, to Havana to Find Out---Lee Asks for an Immediate Court of Inquiry---Capt. Sigsbee's Suspicions.

CAPT. SIGSBEE, IN A SUPPRESSED DESPATCH TO THE STATE DEPARTMENT, SAYS THE ACCIDENT WAS MADE POSSIBLE BY AN ENEMY

Dr. E. C. Pendleton, Just Arrived from Havana, Says He Overheard Talk There of a Plot to Blow Up the Ship---Capt. Zalinski, the Dynamite Expert, and Other Experts Report to The World that the Wreck Was Not Accidental---Washington Officials Ready for Vigorous Action if Spanish Responsibility Can Be Shown---Divers to Be Sent Down to Make Careful Examinations.

In 1898 the sinking of the battleship Maine *sparked the Spanish-American War.*

After the Spanish-American War, troops from the United States occupied Cuba.

bloody race and class war pitted poor blacks against the wealthier whites of Spanish descent. U.S. marines intervened during these and other crises.

Although the Platt Amendment was canceled in 1934, its authoritarian spirit continues to vex Cubans who see it as a blight on their nation's history. Journalist Carlos Franqui wrote that the Cuban republic "was born deformed because it existed in order to produce sugar and wealth for U.S. investors."

In 1920, the price of sugar fell and Cuba suffered an economic crisis. Hardship, unemployment, and corruption by local government officials were on the rise. In 1925, Gerardo Machado was elected president after promising the people he would improve conditions. Machado did not keep his promises; instead, he became a dictator. He suspended freedom of speech and freedom of the press, and he awarded high-paying government jobs to his blatantly corrupt friends. After 1928, Machado's regime grew more violent. Those who criticized or opposed him were treated harshly. Many were imprisoned or killed. Cubans began fleeing to the United States to escape Machado's bloody reign of terror. The United States wanted Machado out of power but was reluctant to launch yet another open military intervention into Cuban affairs. Instead, U.S. officials quietly gave their support to elements within Cuba that sought to overthrow Machado. In 1933, the combination of a general strike by workers and a military coup led by an army sergeant named Fulgencio Batista forced Machado out of office and out of the country.

The Batista Era

Fulgencio Batista y Zaldívar has been described by historian Robert D. Crassweller as a "very obscure . . . barber, vegetable seller, farmer, stenographer and sergeant." Born to a poor family in 1901, Batista grew up in the rural province of Oriente, home to the majority of Cuba's sugar plantations and also to many of the island's blacks, from whom he was, in part, descended. Friends called him *el mulato lindo*, "the handsome mulatto." Batista's charm and intelligence served him well after he joined the army in 1921; although uneducated, he soon developed a loyal following of soldiers who boosted him to power in 1933.

During the seven years between Batista's coup and his own election to public office, five different men assumed Cuba's presidency, yet Batista alone remained the nation's true commander in chief. This era produced only a single genuine rival for Batista, Ramón Grau San Martín—a liberal university professor and physician who claimed the allegiance of a politically cru-

Cubans in New York City demonstrate against the presidency of Gerardo Machado in 1933.

cial sector of Cuban society, the student activists. Early in Batista's tenure, Grau won appointment to the presidency, but he lasted only four months before being replaced by the first in a series of four puppet presidents.

Meanwhile, Batista took command of Cuba. From 1934 to 1940 he served the country well by improving health care, building schools, and instituting a massive public works program that led to the construction of parks and museums. In addition, Batista instituted a minimum work wage and legalized labor unions.

In 1940 Batista supported a nationwide call for a constitutional convention, an assembly that produced a blueprint for a democratic and progressive government. In that year Cubans held their first free elections and chose Batista as their new president. When his term ended in 1944, Batista complied with the constitution—which forbade consecutive terms in office—and ceded the presidency to his old political adversary: Ramón Grau San Martín. Although he obeyed the letter of the law, Batista did not ultimately honor Cuban democracy. After leaving for Florida in 1944, he retained close ties to his supporters at home, biding his time in the United States until he could reestablish his power in Cuba.

In 1938 Fulgencio Batista (second from left) visited Washington, D.C., and posed for a photograph with Cuban and American dignitaries.

Batista's popularity dwindled in his absence from Cuba, but his desire to rule remained as strong as ever. He returned to Cuba, entered the 1952 presidential race and for a time ignored the widespread prediction that he would fail to win a majority vote. But three weeks before the election Batista realized he could never take power by legal means and so staged a coup d'état. The nation rebelled against this flagrant disregard for democracy, a protest Batista answered with the false promise of free elections in 1953. For the next seven years, Cubans lived in the grip of repression, terrorism, and censorship.

In 1957 Fidel Castro (fourth from left) stands in the Sierra Maestra Mountains with his revolutionary troops.

The Early Castro

Many Cubans responded to Batista's treachery by joining opposition forces, the most idealistic of which was the Ortodoxo party, a group that had formed during the 1930s in opposition to the Machado regime. Since

Cuban peasants often aided Castro by supplying his soldiers with food and shelter.

1947 this coalition had included among its members a University of Havana law student named Fidel Castro. The son of a wealthy plantation owner, Castro had been educated in a prestigious Jesuit school where, as one of his classmates later remembered, "the Jesuits were training him to be the white hope of the right."

Castro, however, had already begun forming his own political beliefs. In 1940, at the age of 14, he tried to organize a strike of the approximately 500 workers on his father's sugar plantation. Five years later he entered the University of Havana and immediately took up with revolutionary student groups. According to the historian Hugh Thomas, "Elections in student politics at Havana were often settled by fists, guns, and kidnappings." Gang violence ruled the university campus, and the assassination of student leaders shocked no one.

By the time of his graduation in 1950 Fidel Castro had received a thorough education in radicalism. Although he married, had a son, and practiced law privately in Havana, he never left the world of politics and gradually worked his way into the leadership of the Ortodoxo party's left wing—a group that violently objected to Batista's sabotaging of democracy in Cuba. In summer 1953, Castro decided to move into action. As he later explained: "When none of the [Ortodoxo] leaders showed they had the ability, the resolution, the seriousness of purpose to overthrow Batista, . . . I finally worked out a strategy of my own."

Castro planned an attack on the Moncada military garrison, located near the city of Santiago in Oriente province—the birthplace of both Batista and Castro and a traditional center of revolution in Cuba. The Ortodoxos hoped the siege would serve a twofold purpose—supplying them with arms for a full-scale revolution and sparking an anti-Batista revolt that would first ignite Oriente and then spread throughout Cuba. On July 26, 1953, 111 men and 2 women stormed Moncada. Although the 1,000 soldiers there resisted the assault—and captured Castro, among others—the events of the day firmly established Castro as an important leader in the fight against Batista.

Exile and Victory

After his arrest, Castro spent two years in a government jail, but imprisonment merely delayed his plans. In May 1955, just weeks after his release, he went to Mexico and set up a camp to train a guerrilla army for action against Batista.

Castro and his followers were by no means Batista's only opponents. Although the wealthiest Cubans tended to support Batista, many liberals among the professionals and the middle class despised the Batista regime both for its corruption and for its betrayal of democracy. Yet there was little they could do: Batista ruthlessly crushed all political opposition, refusing to allow anyone to compete against him in free elections. Many were afraid to speak out against him, fearing that they or their families would be punished. The army—commanded by officers who enjoyed the bribes and privileges Batista provided—firmly backed the dictator. Castro won the initial support of many anti-Batista Cubans because they believed he represented the only thing that could bring them freedom: armed rebellion.

In Mexico, Castro formed an anti-Batista group called the 26th of July movement, named for the date of the Moncada attack. He assembled a group of fierce and devoted followers, including his brother Raul, who was a communist, and an Argentine revolutionary named Ernesto "Che" Guevara. After 18 months of training, they secretly contacted supporters in Cuba and arranged an uprising that was scheduled to erupt in Santiago just as the revolutionaries returned home. On November 25, 1956, Castro and 81 followers boarded the boat *Granma* and set out on a storm-wracked, thousand-mile journey to Cuba.

The trip took longer than expected, and when the seasick revolutionaries came ashore in a swamp they were nearly destroyed by Batista's army, which had learned of the *Granma*'s arrival while suppressing the Santiago uprising. The surviving members of the landing party fled into the Sierra Maestra, a 70-mile strip of jungle-covered mountains in Oriente province, Cuba's poorest and most rugged district. Castro was one of the survivors. He quickly learned the lay of the land and won the trust of the local peasants.

The 26th of July movement attracted new followers and by February 1957 was engaged in a guerrilla war against Batista's army. The guerrillas set fire to sugarcane fields, blew up property, and raided military outposts. When not in active combat, they kept on the move, rarely sleeping in the same place for more than one night. On May 28, 1957, they won their first miliary victory, capturing the El Uvero army garrison and seizing the weapons stored there.

While his forces grew stronger, Castro remained hidden in the mountains, an elusive target for the army. In contrast, revolutionaries in Cuban cities such as Havana, Santiago, and Rosaria often met the full force of Batista's counterterrorist troops. The dictator publicly executed 22 opposition leaders. Some of them were captured members of the 26th of July movement; others belonged to the Ortodoxo party, the Communist party, and other new groups that had boldly formed in defiance of Batista. Batista had thought that the execution of opposition leaders would fortify his rule, but the bloodshed weakened it by strengthening the opposition. Batista's dictatorship was being undermined by terrorism, a seesaw economy, the widening economic gap between urban Cubans and poor country people, and the dissatisfaction of the middle class.

As the government's popularity continued to fall, Castro consolidated his support among all segments of Cuban society. He had already achieved near-mythic status by surviving the Moncada attack and the *Granma* landing, yet he remained a mystery to his fellow Cubans. To some he was a heroic Robin Hood figure; to others he was a dangerous murderer.

Castro's political intentions were murky. Batista called him a communist, but Castro claimed that he was not a communist or a socialist, although many of his followers openly advocated communism. In his speeches he spoke of a vague social order that was "neither capitalism nor socialism, but revolutionary humanism." Castro's cause gained prestige at home and abroad in February 1957, when the *New York Times* published an interview with him that had been conducted in secret by

Castro's rebel army entered Havana in January 1959, to a tumultuous welcome.

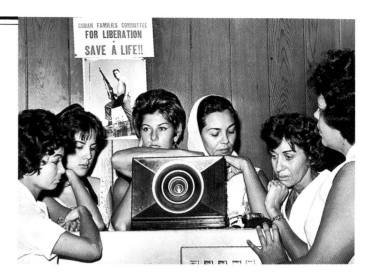

In 1961 Cubans in the United States gather around a radio to await news of the Bay of Pigs invasion.

American journalist Herbert Matthews. The article portrayed Castro as a romantic figure and vastly overestimated the number of his followers. Yet Castro was playing a game of deception that fooled not only Matthews but many other Americans, as well as many Cubans. Although he claimed not to be a communist, the 26th of July movement was powered by a considerable amount of socialist and pro-communist rhetoric, and observers in the U.S. government were fairly certain that Castro's goals were not democratic.

By 1958 many opposition groups—including Cuba's Communist party—had joined forces with Castro, the acknowledged commander-in-chief of the revolutionary movement. Midway through the year, Che Guevara and another Fidelist launched a military campaign to gain control of key cities in Cuba's interior. At the same time, disloyalty surfaced among Batista's troops, especially after the United States significantly weakened the Batista regime by ending its military aid. On January 1, 1959, Batista left Cuba with his wife and a group of followers, escaping by plane to Santo Domingo. Hundreds of Batistianos, as his supporters were called, fled the country in his wake, many traveling by plane to Louisiana and Florida.

The day after Batista's flight, Castro set out on a triumphal march from Santiago to Havana, a 500-mile trek along Cuba's central highway. People camped out along the route to catch a glimpse of Castro, whom one newspaper had already called "the hero-guide of Cuban reform." On January 8, Castro reached the cheering crowds of Havana. People held up signs reading *"Gracias Fidel"* ("Thanks Fidel"). One eyewitness later recalled, "As I watched Castro I realized the magic of his personality. . . . He seemed to weave a hypnotic net over his listeners, making them believe in his own concept of the functions of Government and the destiny of Cuba."

From Rebel to Ruler

The Cubans who welcomed Castro to Havana saw him as a reformer who would clean up the corruption that had plagued Cuban politics for decades. Cubans simply wanted to practice what they already had in principle: a constitutional democracy. Castro himself had described the 26th of July movement as aiming to "achieve all reforms within the spirit and practice of our enlightened Constitution of 1940."

Castro was elected prime minister in February 1959. Within months he introduced a program of socialist economic reforms, bringing the economy under state control. He lowered the prices of meat, medicine, and electricity and seized privately owned land from large estates for redistribution to collectives of peasant farmers. Journalist Carlos Franqui recalls that Castro's supporters and Cuba's poorer people "were delirious with joy and went on a consumer binge. We were having a hell of a time."

But as quickly as Cubans had hailed Castro as their hero, they cursed his policies. His economic plan was based on the typical communist model—he intended to turn Cuba, traditionally an agricultural country, into an industrial nation in which the state would control both industry and agriculture. In redirecting workers to industrial jobs, however, Castro removed too many people from the fields. Agriculture suffered, and a nationwide food shortage resulted.

Castro also failed to keep his promise of participatory democracy. The 26th of July movement ceased to exist when Castro assumed leadership of the country, and the revolutionary leader kept a tight hold on the reins of power. Many Cubans feared his growing dependence upon his brother Raúl and other avowed communists and his increasingly obvious ties with the Soviet Union. Castro sought economic aid from the United States but met with a cool reception, partly because he had seized more than $2 billion worth of U.S.-owned property in Cuba and partly because his regime was already showing clear communist influences. In early 1960, Castro signed a long-term trade agreement with the Soviet Union, which was then the world's communist superpower. Castro tried to force U.S. oil companies that owned refineries in Cuba to process Soviet crude oil; when the U.S. companies refused, Castro seized control of the refineries and declared them Cuban property. The United States and Cuba broke off diplomatic relations in January 1961. Relations between the two countries grew worse during the "Cuban missile crisis" of 1962, when U.S. ships blockaded Cuba, cutting off trade and aid from other countries, until the Soviet Union agreed to remove its long-range missiles from its bases in Cuba.

Food shortages, economic confusion, and Castro's alliance with the communist powers turned many Cubans against him. A flood of refugees began streaming out of Castro's Cuba. The exodus included many of Cuba's best-educated citizens, professionals, intellectuals, and skilled workers who fled to nearby Florida. These Cuban exiles pressured the United States to launch a military invasion of Cuba to overthrow Castro. When the U.S. government resisted this pressure, the exiles—including some of the Batistianos who had fled in 1959—gathered weapons for their own invasion. Their mounting determination to reclaim Cuba paralleled Castro's increasingly open communism.

The United States, engaged in the Cold War to prevent the Soviet Union from achieving its stated goal of global domination, finally yielded to the exiles' demands. President John F. Kennedy approved a plan under which the exiles would receive military training from the Central Intelligence Agency and then invade Cuba with U.S. support. Kennedy and his advisors hoped that the return of the armed exiles would spark a popular uprising against Castro throughout Cuba.

On April 17, 1961, U.S. Brigade 2506—numbering 1,500 Cuban exiles—landed in Cuba's Bay of Pigs, expecting to rout Castro's forces easily. They counted, in part, on the military support of support of U.S. fighter planes promised them by President Kennedy. But Kennedy reneged on his promise at the last minute and left the exiles at the mercy of Castro's large and successful militia, which killed 129 invaders and captured 1,180 prisoners. Flushed with triumph, Castro again threw his gauntlet before the United States by announcing on May 1, 1961, that Cuba was a Marxist-Leninist state.

America's Cuban community rued the failure of the United States to launch a full-scale military invasion of their native country. But their thoughts soon turned to the more immediate concern of the friends and family still living in Cuba. Many who had at first supported Castro found themselves suddenly living in a Communist dictatorship, and because Castro had instituted a ban on emigration, they were stranded in their homeland, just 90 miles from the freedom of American shores. ✖

In October 1962, Cuban refugees gathered to hear President Kennedy address the nation during the Cuban Missile Crisis.

A
SUDDEN
EXILE

P olitical and economic upheavals have driven Cubans to the United States since 1868, when Cuba launched its first war of independence against Spain. During the Ten Years' War, hundreds of Cubans traveled to New York and New Orleans in order to wait out the conflict in safer surroundings. Those migrants who preferred to live closer to their homeland scattered across the Florida islands of Key West, a community that had welcomed Cubans— mostly cigar manufacturers and their employees—since 1831.

Few Cubans intended to settle permanently in the United States, and most regarded their journey to America's shores not as a pilgrimage to a land of opportunity but as a hiatus in their "real" lives, which they fully expected to resume in Cuba. During the 20th century, such stays in the United States became more and more frequent as politics in Cuba grew increasingly chaotic. By the 1930s approximately 34,000 people of Cuban descent, many of them refugees from the vicious reign of President Gerardo Machado, had made their way to American shores. Another mass flight occurred during the last years of Batista's regime, when 10,000 to 15,000 Cubans annually fled their country to come to the United States.

Yet even those sizable numbers prepared no one for the wave of Cubans who left their homeland during and after 1959. Nearly 3,000 of Cuba's political elite left the country immediately after Batista's downfall. Privileged and powerful, many of these "golden exiles" had made fortunes from the casinos, prostitutes, and drugs that characterized Havana in the 1950s—profits that they had protected by investing in foreign banks. They escaped not to save their property but their lives, for they knew that if Castro caught them he would show little mercy. These Batistianos, who abhorred Castro and his revolutionary ideals, had every intention of toppling his rule someday. In fact, many helped organize the Bay of Pigs invasion in 1961.

Not all wealthy Cubans opposed Castro, however. He at first commanded the respect of the country's upper classes, including traditionally conservative groups such as ranchers, plantation owners, and cigar manufacturers—people who gained nothing from Batista's corruption and longed for social stability. Yet just a year into the new regime, many from this same group followed the Batistianos to American shores.

Many Havana casinos paid kickbacks to President Batista in return for an operating license.

The Flight of the Middle Class

By 1960 Castro had begun to nationalize privately owned businesses, a process that in some cases amounted to theft. Often government agents arrived without prior warning to tell a surprised business owner that his company was now the property of the government. One victim of the new policy voiced the dismay of many Cubans when he said that the government "had taken everything away from people who had been able to achieve something with honest work." Unlike the cash-rich Batistianos, Cuba's cattle-raisers, landowners, and manufacturing magnates could not simply send their holdings off to a foreign bank or smuggle them onto an airplane. Most hastily gathered whatever money they had and left the country with only a fraction of their worldly goods.

Some business owners faced not only the confiscation of their property but also punishment for the crime of being "too capitalistic." The experience of Eugene

A prosperous Cuban family poses for a group portrait in the late 1950s.

During the early 1960s, Soviet-built tanks frequently rolled through Havana, panicking the Cuban populace.

Ramos and David Egonzi—one the manager of a shoe factory, the other a shoe wholesaler—typified that of many upper middle-class Cubans. In 1960, Ramos and Egonzi both faced imprisonment and decided to escape Cuba. They knew, however, that their lives in America would be miserable unless they could bring enough of their savings to begin a new company there. With the help of professional smugglers—whom they paid 25 percent of all they owned—Ramos and Egonzi arrived in the United States with enough capital to finance a new business, the Suave Shoe Corporation.

After appropriating the holdings of the wealthy, Castro set his sights on Cuba's professional class. Judges, lawyers, accountants, and doctors—many of whom owned no property worth redistributing—fell victim to the new drive to politicize Cuba. One judge decided to emigrate after receiving an official order to write "Fatherland or Death" after his signature on all legal documents. A Cuban accountant remembers the chaos caused by Cuba's rapid transformation into a communist society: "We dedicated ourselves to family, work and friends . . . . Then suddenly a brutal change came into our lives. Our democratic, religious, and cultural institutions were crushed overnight. There was complete disunity in the Cuban family."

The disorder in Cuban society cut across class lines, panicking office workers, embroiderers, teachers, and civil servants, as well as bankers and doctors. Families were wrenched apart and neighbor turned against neighbor. Each residential district, for example, housed a Committee for the Defense of the Revolution, an organization that inventoried people's belongings and kept accounts of their comings and goings. Political neutrality was impossible: those who were not avowed communists were called *gusanos*, or "worms." Cuban-American writer Reinaldo Arenas described the mood of this era in his novel *Farewell to the Sea*:

> everything seems to be crumbling, rotting . . . and only poverty, fear, incessant harassment remain. Today they abolished such and such a program, yesterday they suppressed such and such a magazine, today they rationed such and such a product, yesterday they arrested such and such a person, today the firing squad executed so many people. Yesterday, today, on and on and on, until the terrible becomes merely monotonous.

No Cubans living through this time could know what the future held. Some believed that the state would claim responsibility for their children, whereas others predicted the schools would abandon traditional subjects in favor of communist doctrine. Many parents decided to send their sons and daughters abroad rather than run the risk of losing them to the government. During the early 1960s nearly 14,000 children were sent alone to the United States by parents who could not themselves leave Cuba. During the same period—from about 1959 to 1962—the total number of Cuban exiles was more than 155,000.

A Tightening Grip

Many Cubans agonized over the decision to leave their homeland, but, until the summer of 1961, they could do so with relative ease by booking any of 12,000 seats available each month on Pan American Airlines flights to Miami. Castro at first presented few barriers to those

Cubans wishing to emigrate during the early 1960s sometimes were allowed only a few days to assemble essential documents.

wanting to leave and was even glad to see them go. He later explained:

> In this country when we say to someone "If you want to leave, we aren't going to stop you, you are free to leave," this country doesn't lose a citizen . . . . Because that citizen could never be considered—from our revolutionary point of view, from our Marxist point of view—a [true] citizen of this country.

After the Bay of Pigs invasion in May 1961, however, Castro saw voluntary emigration as an insufficient means of "purging" those who might be disloyal to the Marxist-Leninist state of Cuba. He grew violently suspicious of any Cubans wanting to escape his rule and detained or jailed many instead of simply allowing them to leave the country.

As Castro's grip on the nation tightened, more Cubans wanted to flee. Many people who had neither supported Batista nor opposed Castro found themselves imprisoned for no apparent reason. One office worker later remembered, "When the [security forces] arrested me and all of my family just because we were [practicing] Catholics, I realized that there was no security for any kind of man. I decided to leave." The communist victory in fighting American-backed troops convinced many people that unlike previous Cuban leaders who had quickly risen to power, Castro would endure. In the words of one former journalist, "I decided to leave Cuba because the absurd failure of [Bay of Pigs] showed me that the situation in Cuba had reached the point where the communist domination of my country would last for at least two more years."

After the spring of 1961, the hardship worsened for Cubans who were granted permission to leave their country. All potential exiles had to turn over their savings to the Cuban government and were allowed to keep only five dollars in American money, one suit of clothing, and a few changes of underwear. Yet even such harsh regulations could not stem the tide of the 1,600

(continued on page 57)

(Overleaf) Cuban-American men play dominoes in a Little Havana park.

*Cuban Americans have carried the politics, art, and industry of their
homeland to the United States. At a rally in Florida, Cuban immigrants
wave the flags of their native and adopted countries; two performers
personify the vibrant nightlife of prerevolutionary Havana; and cigar rollers
practice a traditional Cuban craft.*

Two walls in Little Havana—one bearing anti-Castro graffiti, the other depicting a scene from colonial Cuba—reflect the community's history. So too does Gilberto Puiz's Good News Call (opposite).

Cuban-born painter Paul Sierra portrays the traumas of persecution and exile in such haunting works as Mad Dogs *(above),* Disappearing Memories *(above, left), and* Under Another Sky *(below, left).*

In Facades, *Cuban-American artist Carlos Maciá mixes pencil and watercolors to create a bizarre tableau.*

Newly arrived immigrants in Florida await "processing" by United States authorities.

(continued from page 48)
to 1,800 Cubans—men and women from all walks of life—who boarded Miami-bound airplanes each week.

The wave of Cuban emigration would probably have continued at this rate but was curtailed by the crisis that arose between Cuba and the United States. In October 1962, President Kennedy ordered a naval blockade of Cuba after learning that the Soviet Union had supplied that country with nuclear-armed missiles. Although the Soviets soon agreed to remove the missiles, the incident widened the rift between Cuba and the United States. All air flights to and from Miami were discontinued and emigration from Cuba was banned. Nevertheless approximately 30,000 Cubans managed to make their way secretly to America, some crossing the waters between their country and Florida by boat. Those with enough money usually flew first to Spain or Mexico and then entered the United States from there.

Varadero and Mariel

During the next three years growing discontent touched all segments of Cuban society. Castro had instituted a rationing program in order to counter a nationwide food shortage. Although Cubans had a ready supply of coupons entitling them to buy groceries, the food itself was

In June 1980 this shrimp-fishing boat, the Lady Mary, *left the Port of Mariel for Key West, Florida, laden with refugees.*

scarce and people feared starvation. The panic turned some of Castro's staunchest supporters—members of the working class—against him. When the doors of emigration again opened in 1965—after President Lyndon Johnson and Castro signed a "memorandum of understanding" between their two nations—a broad spectrum of Cuban society welcomed the possibility of leaving Castro's regime. That September Castro announced that people with family members in the United States were free to join them.

A mass exodus from Cuba to the United States soon overwhelmed the governments of both countries. Hundreds of Cuban exiles had sailed from Florida to the port of Camarioca to pick up boatloads of their relatives and bring them to America. Castro and Johnson realized that the flow of migrants had to be controlled and so created a system that accorded preferential rights of immigration first to spouses, second to parents, and third to siblings of United States residents. The two countries agreed also to allow regularly scheduled plane flights between Varadero (a beach in Cuba) and Miami, Florida—an airlift that brought 3,700 Cubans to the United States each month.

Though the doors to freedom had been opened, they swung back into the faces of many hopeful emigrants. Isabel Gonzalez, a Cuban woman who now lives in New Jersey, waited four years and four months for permission to leave her native country, yet she had to remain in Cuba only half as long as many of her friends and neighbors. Some Cubans not only endured long periods of uncertainty but fell into disfavor with the government once they announced their intention to emigrate and were forced to perform "voluntary labor"—sometimes for as long as two years—while the authorities decided their fate. Such delays disappointed the plans of many potential emigrants, who saw Castro outlaw the airlift in 1973 while they were still months away from receiving authorization to leave the country.

During the next seven years Castro again restricted Cuban emigration. Cubans had virtually no legal means of entering the United States and often resorted to extreme measures—such as voyaging across the Straits of Florida in homemade boats—to reach America. One dramatic attempt at escape inadvertently touched off the next wave of Cuban emigration to the United States. In March 1980, a group of Cubans crashed through the gates of the Peruvian embassy in Havana and asked to be granted political asylum in Peru. Three days later the Cuban government announced that all those who wanted to leave the island could gather at the embassy, an invitation that drew a crowd of 11,000.

Although this public expression of dissatisfaction did not reflect well on Castro, he quickly turned the situation into a political victory over the United States. Earlier that month American president Jimmy Carter had signed into law the Refugee Act of 1980, an immigration bill that narrowed the definition of "refugee." Under the old law anyone escaping from a communist country automatically qualified for asylum in the United States. The new act required that exiles seeking asylum be subject to or threatened by political, racial, or religious persecution in their homeland.

The U.S. government counted on these new restrictions to stem the tide of refugees from Cuba, Haiti, and other impoverished countries from which most citizens with money, skills, and professional educations had already fled.

In April 1980, Castro responded to the tremendous turnout at the Peruvian embassy by opening Cuba's port of Mariel to any Cubans who wanted to emigrate to the United States. Despite discouragement from the United States, about 125,000 Cubans entered the country from April to October of 1980. Many of these Marielitos, as those leaving from Mariel were called, arrived in the United States without proper visas or identification. The majority made the journey to Florida on privately owned fishing or excursion boats that charged high prices for the trip. This "boatlift" was dangerous; many of the vessels were unseaworthy or overcrowded. A May 1980 issue of *Time* magazine reported, "More than 20 Cubans have died in the journey so far, including three last week who had crowded with 27 others into a small cabin on the 36-foot cruiser *Sunshine*. Two of them died of suffocation, and one from engine exhaust fumes."

The Marielitos were different from the earlier waves of Cuban immigrants. About 1,700 of them were convicted criminals or mentally ill persons; Castro had emptied prisons and mental hospitals and sent their occupants to the United States as a cynical trick, a way of shifting his own problems over to his enemy. The Marielitos undoubtedly introduced a criminal element into the Cuban-American population. Linda Chavez, author of *Out of the Barrio*, wrote in 1991 that 4,000 Marielitos were then serving time in prison for crimes committed in the United States.

There were also racial and economic differences between the Marielitos and the earlier Cuban immigrants. Ninety percent of the earlier immigrants had been white. About a third of the Marielitos, however, were of Afro-Cuban descent. Their arrival brought to the Cuban-American community a racial diversity that more closely resembled that of Cuba's population. The Marielitos also broadened the class diversity among

Cubans in America. A majority of the earlier immigrants had been from the upper or middle classes—educated, professional people or skilled workers or wealthy owners of land or businesses. Many of the Marielitos, however, were poor and comparatively uneducated and unskilled. Cuban society had traditionally placed significant emphasis on class, and it was the difference in social and economic standing, more than racial differences, that prevented the earlier immigrants from welcoming the Marielitos with open arms. Some longtime residents of "Little Havana" in Miami vehemently opposed the Marielitos' arrival. Nevertheless, most Marielitos succeeded in entering the United States. Many had trouble getting jobs because they lacked education and skills; within a year of their arrival, about 25 percent of them were receiving support from welfare programs. But the Marielitos shared the ethic of self-sufficiency and hard work that characterizes other Cuban immigrants, and within three years 15 percent of them had started their own businesses and another 13 percent had entered technical or professional occupations, according to a study by Alejandro Portes and Robert Bach, reported in *Out of the Barrio.*

Marielitos often crammed into small boat cabins during passage to the United States.

In 1987 Augustin Roman, the Auxiliary Bishop of Miami, serves holy communion to a prisoner at a federal detention center.

A New Era

The hardship endured by those Marielitos granted refugee status in America seems small in comparison to that suffered by the 2,746 who never gained permission to freely enter the country. Immediately after the Mariel exodus Castro agreed to accept the rejected emigrants back into Cuba, but, in fact, he allowed only 201 to return to their native land before rescinding his promise and thus sentencing 2,545 Cubans to indefinite imprisonment in the United States.

For seven years Marielitos languished in federal detention centers in Atlanta, Georgia, and Oakdale, Louisiana, while civil rights groups such as the American Civil Liberties Union tried in vain to free them. In November 1987 their crisis came to a head when the U.S. government announced that it would restore its 1980 immigration agreement with Cuba, an accord that allowed the United States to deport the detainees back to their homeland. Inmates at both Federal detention centers balked when they received word of the new settlement between Cuba and the United States: The 1,120 prisoners in Atlanta rioted and took 94 hostages. Two days later approximately 1,000 Marielitos in Oakdale seized control of their detention center and kept 26 federal employees prisoner.

Negotiations between the Marielitos and prison officials proceeded slowly in both Atlanta and Oakdale. Many believed they would have been stalemated indefinitely if not for the intervention of Auxiliary Bishop Augustin A. Roman, the highest ranking Hispanic priest in the archdiocese of Miami. According to a *New York Times* article, "[Roman] is a man who has never forgotten his humble roots." Born in 1929 to a poor family in Cuba, Roman studied in seminaries in Mantanas, Cuba, and Quebec, Canada. He returned to his native country in order to champion the poor, but in 1961 he met the opposition of Fidel Castro, who banished him from Cuba.

At first Roman relocated in Chile where, under the aegis of the Roman Catholic church, he worked to improve the lives of that region's poor Indians. At the end of the decade the priest again pulled up his roots, this time settling in Miami, Florida, where he built the Ermita de la Caridad, his parish church and a shrine dedicated to the patron saint of Cuba. Yet Roman was determined to serve not only established Cuban Americans but also those who were reviled by the community at large. In March 1987 he defended the rights of the Marielitos by saying, "It is a basic right that after a man or a woman has paid his or her debt to society his or her freedom should be restored." According to the *New York Times*:

> Roman has frequently raised his low but firm voice in defense of the downtrodden, including political prisoners in Cuba and the Mariel boatlift detainees in the United States . . . . During [the November 1987 riots] rebellious inmates requested a meeting with him and religious leaders suggested that he serve as an intermediary between Federal authorities and the detainees.

The bishop helped forge an accord between the two sides, thus ending both prison takeovers by early December. The government agreed to review the case of each Marielito individually instead of herding the group back to Cuba en masse. Although the riots received a mixed response from Cuban Americans, the community as a whole agreed that the prisoners had dramatized their revulsion for the Castro regime and their conviction that no matter what fate held for them in the United States, it was preferable to what they might face in Cuba.

Cuban inmates in Oakdale, Louisiana, celebrate the signing of a deportation agreement with the United States government in November 1987.

A
NEW HOME

When Cuban immigrants first stepped onto American soil, most did so in Miami, Florida—a city that lay only 150 miles from their homeland. Since the 1870s, Cubans have resettled in Miami, where the balmy climate and easy pace of life reminded them of home. By the late 1950s the city could claim approximately 46,000 people of Cuban origin, including students, retirees, political exiles, and workers in American or Cuban-owned businesses—a population that established Miami as a Cuban stronghold in the United States. In a *New Yorker* article entitled "The Second Havana" author David Rieff wrote:

> In Miami, Cuba is with you everywhere. Its presence can be felt immediately by the traveller arriving at the Miami International Airport. The predominant language of passersby there is Spanish. Over the public-address system, many flight announcements are routinely made in both Spanish and English . . . . And in Miami the Spanish that one hears is neither schooled Castillian nor the leisurely accents of Mexico but, rather, that fast, jolting Cuban variant of the language which was once described as . . . "Spanish in overdrive."

After the revolution of 1959 Florida's prospering Cuban-American community swelled to unforeseen proportions as the "golden exiles" of Batista's regime spilled into Miami, bringing their families and their riches with them. One expert has estimated that this elite brought at least $20 million into greater Miami, enough to buy up the entire town. But even that vast sum could neither support nor create enough jobs and housing for the nearly 1,600 refugees who streamed into the city each week during the early 1960s.

The magnitude of the Cuban migration caught the U.S. government by surprise and in particular captured the attention of President Dwight Eisenhower. In 1959 he assigned Tracy Vorhees, a lawyer who had directed the Hungarian refugee program of the late 1950s, to aid the Cuban exiles who thronged Miami.

Vorhees began by obtaining proper visas for the immigrants so that they could legally remain in the United States. Many had left Cuba so hastily that they lacked the proper documentation to apply for U.S. residency. Others had applied only for tourist visas because they expected to stay temporarily in the United States until the situation at home "cleared." Tourist visas carried a 30-day limit and prohibited permanent employment for those who carried them. Vorhees persuaded the Im-

A photograph from 1951 shows Miami's Biscayne Boulevard, long home to some of America's most luxurious hotels.

migration and Naturalization Service to grant the Cuban exiles special permission to work in the United States. In addition, he successfully lobbied Congress to pass a law granting Cubans permanent residency in America—their first step toward obtaining citizenship.

In 1960 the U.S. government—in response to Vorhees's advice—established the Cuban Refugee Emergency Center in Miami, a shelter and meeting place that assisted 77 percent of all those arriving from Cuba in 1960–63. The center provided Cubans with temporary housing ("freedom beds"), up to $100 a month in aid, medical care, meals, and even educational loans. Those Cubans who eventually found homes near this haven could visit regularly for English language lessons, job counseling, and companionship.

The center helped immigrants settle in Miami, but it also rechanneled them to other parts of the country so that the city—still a small one in the early 1960s—would not burst at the seams. The center started a relocation program that gave exiles incentives to live and work in other parts of America. One of the beneficiaries of this program was Luis Padilla.

In 1961 Padilla, his wife, and their two small sons arrived in Miami—via Jamaica—from Havana, where Padilla had headed the legal department of Cuba's Federal Health and Administration service. Padilla moved his family into an apartment and began work as a dishwasher and desk clerk in a small hotel, where he labored 10 hours a day, including Saturday and Sunday, for a salary of $27 a week. At that time many American businesses were failing in Miami, and Padilla considered himself fortunate to have any job at all.

Padilla and his wife fed the family with surplus food they received from a U.S. government warehouse. He recalled, "They kept giving us peanut butter. Cubans hate peanut butter but there was more and more of it. Also they gave us navy beans, but not the black beans we were used to." The Padillas' plight worsened when his wife became pregnant with their third child. "I had no money to pay the medical bills, so I went to the

A mother and daughter stand in front of the Cuban Refugee Emergency Center in Miami.

In 1987 Luis Padilla retired from the 3M Company after a career that spanned three decades.

refugee center. They asked me if I had a job, and if I worked eight hours a day. I told them I worked 10 hours a day but made only $27 a week, but they said they could not help me because I already had permanent employment. A few days later I got a call from the center. They said that they would help with medical aid if I signed papers and agreed to relocate anywhere in the United States."

The Padillas soon found that "anywhere" was St. Paul, Minnesota. Luis Padilla's first new position was that of janitor in a macaroni factory, but soon he was able put his professional training to use when he won a job as a researcher in the legal department of one of America's largest corporations, the Minnesota Mining and Manufacturing Company (3M). While working full time, Padilla also studied for the bar examination that would qualify him to practice law in the United States.

In 1967 Padilla gained admittance to the Minnesota Bar Association and began his career in earnest, rising from researcher to lawyer to Senior Associate-Counsel—a position he still holds—during the next two decades. Although the Padillas still visit their relatives in Miami, they have settled permanently in Minnesota and there raised three sons, one of whom now practices law.

The Workaday World

The Refugee Center relocation program boasted many success stories similar to that of Luis Padilla, but the majority of its approximately 50,000 participants returned to Miami within a year of their move. Although New York, Chicago, and other cities offered better jobs and higher salaries, they could not provide immigrants with compatriots who would drink *cafecitas* (Cuban demitasse) and discuss politics with them at a local café. Despite its drawbacks, Miami still offered reminders of life in Havana.

Cubans accepted jobs wherever they could find them in order to remain in Florida, usually in the resort hotels that drew millions of American tourists southward each year. By the early 1970s hotel staffs were almost 50 percent Cuban. Men and women who had once defended clients in courtrooms or run government agencies now carried luggage or washed dishes in Miami restaurants. Cubans soon earned a reputation as energetic and responsible workers. In 1961 the chief of the Catholic Relief Service's resettlement division told *Time* magazine: "The one thing you notice is [the Cubans'] willingness to work. They just want a job, whether it be as a porter or a dishwasher. They know they have to start at the bottom of the totem pole."

Cubans retained their pride despite their menial employment. Families insisted on supporting themselves

Two patrons pause in front of a Cuban restaurant in downtown Miami.

Cuban immigrants iron clothing in a Florida garment factory.

and taking money from charities or the U.S. government only when absolutely necessary. Throughout the 1960s the Cuban Refugee Center received up to $10,000 a month from exiles who had resettled and wanted to pay back the loans they had once needed in order to survive.

And many Cubans eventually regained their former social status. Carlos Arboleya was working as the chief auditor of Cuba's largest bank when Castro nationalized the country's banks in October 1960. "I resigned the same day," he said. "I believed too strongly in freedom

and democracy and the free enterprise system. I defi-
nitely could not work for a Communist regime." Arboleya decided to emigrate, entered the United States
with only $40, and was forced to work as an inventory
clerk in a shoe factory. Within 18 months he had assumed the vice-presidency of the company but still
missed the world of finance. After six more years he
landed a job in a bank, as president of Fidelity National
of South Miami.

During the 1960s an increasing number of Cubans
established themselves in Miami and they, in turn,
hired other Cubans to work for them. All in all, business seemed the easiest profession for Cubans to break
into; law and medicine the hardest. Although many
American hospitals suffered from a general shortage of
physicians during the early 1960s, they hired Cuban
doctors only as medical technicians. Approximately
2,000 Cubans with medical degrees suffered from un-
deremployment until President Kennedy suggested that
the University of Miami tutor them for a licensing examination required of all foreign-trained doctors. The
university's 12-week refresher course enabled about
half the physicians enrolled to pass the test and begin
practicing medicine.

The Boomtown Era

Cuban exiles gradually began to make inroads into middle-class professions. The community as a whole benefited both from the scattered achievements of
individuals and from an economic transformation that
affected every resident of Miami and turned all eyes
toward the city's Cuban-American community. In his
article, "The Second Havana," David Rieff explains:

> The real key to the Cuban success in Miami and,
> insofar as the two are separable, to the success of the
> city as a whole is that in Miami not only is Cuba with
> you wherever you turn but so is Latin America. Cuban-
> Americans in Miami quickly spotted the increasing

American trade with Latin America—part of a fundamental economic shift in the nineteen-sixties by which the United States became far more closely connected with Latin America than it had ever been before—and presented themselves as middlemen. They spoke Spanish . . . and they had experience in doing business with Latin Americans.

Cuban Americans served as a link between the business community of Latin America and that of the United States, which began trading more frequently with South American countries during the 1960s. The Cubans shared the language and some of the culture of such oil-rich countries as Venezuela and easily established a rapport with Venezuelan businessmen, who preferred Miami's Cuban bankers to the remote financiers of New York's Wall Street. Venezuelans boosted Miami's economy not only by using local banks but by spending their vacations in the city's resort hotels and their cash on local real estate. During the recession of the mid-1970s, Miami was the only major U.S. city with an increase in per capita income, a boom it owed to its Cuban Americans.

Bilingual signs are a common sight in Miami.

Miami's new economic vitality—linked to Latin America—has been reflected in the growth of the city's ethnic neighborhoods and in its cultural life. Little Havana kept getting bigger during the 1980s, and communities of immigrants from Nicaragua, Venezuela, and other Latin American countries also formed. Miami's restaurants, boutiques, performing arts centers, and radio stations reflected the strong Latin American influence, still dominated by Cuban Americans. The city's Latin American boom ushered in a general revival, in which landmark hotels and other buildings from the 1920s and 1930s—many of them decorated in

The Our Lady of Charity processional moves along Bergenline Avenue in Union City, New Jersey.

A Cuban American reads el Herald, *a Spanish-language edition of The* Miami Herald. *The publication was superseded by* el Nuevo Herald *in 1987.*

an architectural style called Art Deco—were renovated and restored. Largely due to its Latin American flair, Miami began to play a larger role in the fashion, film and television, and music industries.

By the 1970s, Cubans had become a significant presence in Miami's service industry and its small-business community. Between 1960 and 1979, for example, the percentage of Hispanic-owned gas stations rose from 12 to 48 percent. Cuban Americans also bought laundromats, dry-cleaning shops, and grocery stores. Many started or purchased their businesses with help from the Small Business Administration (SBA). Between 1968 and 1979, Cubans received approximately $47 million worth of SBA loans.

The Spanish language began resounding through Miami, for the Cuban immigrants had brought their native tongue to the United States. Most of them spoke and read only Spanish. By the 1980s, Miami had two Spanish-language television stations, six Spanish radio stations, and a weekly magazine, a daily newspaper, and several tabloids, all printed in Spanish and owned and operated by the Cuban exile community. But mainstream publications in Dade County also wanted to attract some of the area's 720,000 Cubans as readers. In 1987, the Miami *Herald* launched a Spanish-language section of the newspaper called *el Nuevo Herald*, a "paper within the paper" that featured articles and columns by an independent staff of Spanish-speaking journalists. Miami had become a bilingual city, and local ordinances required all public documents, notices, and forms to be printed in both English and Spanish.

Cuban Americans in other U.S. cities have not generally fared as well economically as those in Miami, but they seem to have done as well as other immigrant groups. The Cuban-American population of Union City, New Jersey, numbered about 25,000 people in the mid-1970s and was the largest concentration of Cuban Americans outside Miami. Union City's immigrants tended to follow the standard pattern in this working-class city, seeking jobs in the nearby factories. Some Cuban entrepreneurs bought floundering or defunct businesses on Bergenline Avenue—Union City's commercial thoroughfare—and revitalized a dying district with such stores as the Havana Bakery.

Despite the vast differences between industrial Union City, New Jersey, and sleek Miami, Florida, Cuban Americans in both cities share a common history and attitude. Those of Union City would agree with a 1968 survey taken among Miami's exiles that revealed that what they most missed in the United States were family and domestic life, the homeland, jobs, and "the Cuban way of life." Cubans in New Jersey, Florida, and elsewhere would probably also agree that the secret of happiness in America lay not merely in gaining political or economic power, but in the preservation of families and friendships—ties that have given Cuban Americans the strength to rebuild their lives in a new country. ❧

A woman hawks T-shirts in a Cuban refugee camp in South Florida.

Two
SETS
OF VALUES

As a group, Cubans in the United States rarely stray from the enclaves they established during the 1960s. The La Cubana bus line—a travel service owned by Cuban Americans—shuttles between metropolitan New York; the New Jersey cities of Union and Elizabeth; Washington, D.C.; and Miami. These routes along the East Coast link smaller Cuban-American communities with Dade County, Florida, the stronghold of Cuban exiles in the United States. Although some immigrants dispersed throughout America just after their arrival, the majority returned within months to the familiarity of Miami.

Exiles from Castro's regime eased their transition into America by re-creating as fully as possible the "good life" they had enjoyed at home, even calling their Miami neighborhood "Little Havana." David Rieff writes:

When the Cuban refugees began arriving in South Florida, they carried with them the ashes of bourgeois Havana. They no more meant to adapt to an alien environment than a person who drives his house trailer across a county line means to live in a different house . . . . The Calle Ocho, as it is called by Cuban and Anglo alike, is the central business street of Little Havana . . . . It is where the favored restaurants are and the Cuban radio stations, with their intense blend

In Union City, New Jersey, women prepare to march in a parade celebrating their Cuban heritage.

of Latin music and ferociously right-wing politics; and the businessmen's clubs; and many of the professional offices . . . . Many of the men there, wearing guayabera shirts and sipping endless cups of Cuban coffee, look just as they would on the Prado in downtown Havana.

Cuban immigrants clung to their families and native culture rather than embracing the customs of their new country—and soon earned a reputation for clannishness. A majority of Cuban exiles saw that assimilation would distance them from what they cherished most, *la Cuba de ayer*, the Cuba of yesterday—a land of Old World tradition that seemed truly civilized in comparison with the hurly-burly of life in America. Before the revolution of 1959, for example, most upper-class Cuban boys, and even Castro himself, received a rigorous education in private Catholic schools run by Jesuit priests. During vacations they sometimes took deep-sea fishing trips around Cuba's northern islands or roamed the family sugar plantation on horseback.

Like their brothers, girls from Cuban families partook in the traditions and rituals of their culture. Young women from all walks of life spent months planning their *quince*, an elaborate celebration of their 15th birthday that marked their formal debut into society—a rite of passage second in importance only to a wedding. Those with wealthy parents spared no expense, frequently hosting gala parties at such elite watering holes as the Havana Yacht Club. Cuban-American photographer Tony Mendoza remembered one such occasion:

> My sister Margarita's debut party was held in an elegant stage set in the courtyard of the Havana Yacht Club. I remember hanging out by the bar and talking with friends about Fidel Castro. Politicians were crooks, we all agreed, and if Fidel ever toppled Batista, he would turn out like all the rest. Three years later, 99 percent of the membership of the Havana Yacht Club, including my family, found themselves living in Miami in drastically reduced circumstances.

Once in America, families such as Mendoza's sought out every possible amenity of *la Cuba de ayer*. Some joined the Big Five Club, an amalgam of Havana's five most prestigious social clubs. Others became members of Miami's 114 civic associations, each of which represented a Cuban township (which numbered 126 in all). Nearly every immigrant family—whether in Little Havana or its northern counterpart, Union City, New Jersey—enjoyed the pleasures of Cuban cuisine and filled their home with the familiar smells of fried plantains and black beans mixed with pork.

Language created a rift between different generations of Cuban Americans. The earliest exiles often insisted that their children speak Spanish, fearing that the younger generation would grow up without a proper knowledge of either the language or the culture of their homeland. Yet Cuban Americans who were born in the United States or who entered the country as small children grew up speaking English and often preferred it to the Spanish of their grandparents and parents. Many families struck a compromise in which children spoke English to one another and Spanish to their elders.

These linguistic divisions within a family often mirrored more profound differences. Most exiles who had arrived in the United States as adults considered themselves Cubans living in America, whereas those who had entered the country as children—or were born in America—regarded themselves as Americans of Cuban descent. As one 16 year old told *Time* magazine "Being a Cuban American [means] having two sets of values. At school we live the American life; at home we try to live as Cubans." Conflict often arose between children, who esteemed the American ideal of independence, and their parents, who gave priority to the well-being of the family and community.

Although many older immigrants adopted American customs, they still maintained traditional values within the family, especially in matters of courtship and marriage. Some staunch traditionalists insisted on chaperoning their teenage daughters, but parents with more modern views were content with the peer "supervision" of a double date. Most adults agreed that children, both male and female, should socialize and marry within the Cuban-American community.

Most Cuban Americans of the younger generation obeyed the dictates of their elders, deferring to age and experience, as was traditional within the community. The adults in a household frequently included not only a mother and father, but also aunts, uncles, and grandparents. Older immigrants were welcomed into the homes of their children and grandchildren and thus escaped the isolation and loneliness that afflicted many of their Anglo counterparts. Many undertook the task of child care and became essential to families with two working parents.

In the public world as well as the private, Cuban Americans showed enormous respect for authority. One police officer, contrasting young Cuban Americans with black and Anglo youths, said, "No Cuban has ever called me 'pig' or 'fuzz.' " Indeed, the immigrant community impressed Miami's law enforcers as singularly law-abiding. During the early 1970s, the city's chief of police observed that Cubans committed only 10 to 12 percent of all crimes although they accounted for a third of the population.

Ethnic Conflicts

Not all Americans welcomed the influx of Cubans to the United States. Like other immigrants from Latin America and elsewhere in the world, Cubans have encountered problems with both black and white Americans.

One source of resentment among African Americans is the fact that Cubans, as a minority in the U.S. population, have benefited from affirmative action programs that were designed to help U.S.-born minorities—particularly blacks—obtain jobs and government contracts for goods and services. The Cubans have been, in general, more affluent than most other immigrant groups and ethnic or racial minorities. Some blacks therefore feel that Cubans had no need for the assistance and programs that were meant to help poor blacks.

In Dade County, Florida, some African Americans have felt that the economic success of the Cubans has been won at their expense. When Cuban immigrants began entering Miami in the 1960s, they found jobs in areas that had previously been dominated by blacks, such as service positions in laundries, hotels, and private homes. Although some black critics have complained that the Cubans were given jobs because white employers were more likely to favor Hispanic than black employees, the reality is that people hired Cuban immigrants, in spite of the fact that most of them spoke little or no English, because they worked hard and performed well. They were highly motivated, with a strong family structure; many possessed high levels of education and skills. The success of the Cubans has not been a matter of lighter-skinned immigrants winning out over black Americans. It is rather a case of highly motivated and

The Cuban-American community encompasses different races and religions. Here Jewish children of Cuban descent pose in the playground of the Temple Emanu-El School in Miami.

educated newcomers competing against people from a lower economic and educational class with fewer literacy and work skills—a question of education and motivation, not of race. The problem is a serious one in many American communities and, unfortunately, it has turned some African Americans against immigrants. The process continues today in Florida and other states, where many Cubans are moving out of the service industry into businesses of their own. The service jobs are increasingly being done by new immigrants from Haiti, who are motivated to work because of a strong family structure and a tradition of self-reliance.

Conflict has also arisen over the issue of language. Black and white Americans alike have expressed dismay at the proliferation of Spanish in public schools, docu-

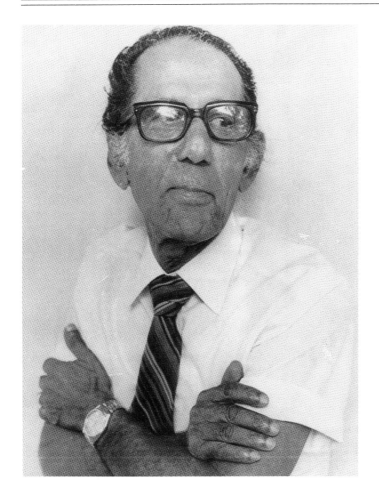

Prisciliano Falcon, who headed the Federation of Sugar Workers in Cuba during the 1950s, has championed the rights of blacks in both Cuba and the United States.

ments, and services. The question of "language rights" is a complex one. Some Hispanic activists insist that the government support their right to speak Spanish by paying for Spanish classes and by introducing bilingualism into all aspects of public life. Yet opponents of bilingualism—including some Hispanics—feel that such policies will lead only to cultural and political fragmentation of the sort that is occurring in Canada, where the French-speaking population of Quebec province has imposed bilingualism on the entire nation. These critics of bilingualism point out that other groups, such as the Greek Americans, have preserved their traditional language at home and in churches and ethnic organizations while still becoming part of the English-speaking mainstream population.

Since the 1980s, several states have passed laws declaring English their "official" language. Floridians voted down a measure to make English the official state language, and Spanish becomes more common there every day. Yet official-English laws have had little or no effect on public policy. In California, where such a law was passed, bilingual instruction continues in public schools and voting ballots and other public documents continue to be printed in Spanish. The question of language—of whether immigrants should be required to learn English, and of whether the United States is to become officially multilingual—will undoubtedly remain a topic of public debate in the years ahead, in Miami and elsewhere.

Cuban immigrants have brought the art of cigar making to the United States.

In 1980 the Bustelo Company provided refugees from Mariel with free cups of cafe cubano while they awaited processing in Miami.

The Political Arena

Cuban Americans made many changes in the course of adjusting to life in America, but most clung fast to their political beliefs—chief of which was a hatred of Castro and communism. A majority of the immigrants joined the Republican party, attracted by the anti-communist stand of President Ronald Reagan during the 1980s. In that decade, the Republican party of Dade County included 73 percent of the region's Cuban Americans. Many were pledged to the cause of liberating Cuba from Castro's rule.

To win support for their struggle, Cuban Americans took the anti-Castro fight to Washington, D.C., where they founded a lobbying organization called the Cuban American Freedom Coalition. The Coalition opposed all pro-communist movements in Latin America. A few Cubans went further; in their zeal to oust Castro, they formed terrorist organizations within the United States. One such extremist group—the Cuban Nationalist Movement, based in Union City, New Jersey—alleg-

In 1981, an FBI agent sorts through weapons confiscated from an anti-Castro terrorist organization.

edly bombed a New Jersey cigar factory after learning that the Cuban-American owner had accepted an invitation from Castro to visit Cuba.

The vast majority of Cuban Americans have no connection with the anti-Castro terrorist groups, yet some agree with their goals. In 1983, a Miami *Herald* poll showed that 22 percent of Cuban Americans in Dade County believed that anti-Castro violence within the United States was justified. That same year, citizens in Miami organized Orlando Bosch Day, in honor of a Cuban who planted a bomb on a Cubana Airlines flight from Venezuela to Havana, killing 73 people. And in August 1987, members of a group called Independent and Democratic Cuba disrupted the Pan American Games in Indianapolis, Indiana, to stage protests against Castro. Some demonstrators tore the Cuban flag and stepped on it, provoking fistfights with the Cuban athletes.

In general, protests against Castro have been organized by older exiles, peers of the Bay of Pigs soldiers. The relationship of these exiles—and the rest of the Cuban-American community—with Cuba has become increasingly complex as political chaos has mounted in Cuba during the 1990s. Restrictions on travel to and from Cuba have begun to ease, and many of the exiles and their children are confronted with the question of whether they should go back to Cuba to visit family members left behind. Many refuse to return as long as Castro remains in power, but the dictator's hold on Cuba is growing shaky. The country's economy is in ruins following the collapse of the Soviet Union, once Cuba's chief benefactor. Many observers predict that the rule of Castro and communism will soon come to an end in Cuba. Cuban Americans are watching events in Cuba closely and thinking about how they will respond when Castro dies or leaves office.

Xavier Suarez, elected mayor of Miami in 1985, represented the values of the new generation of Cuban-American leaders. Born in Las Villas, Cuba, in 1949,

Suarez and his family immigrated to the United States in 1961 and settled in a suburb of Washington, D.C. There Suarez received the Jesuit education typical for a middle-class Cuban boy and after graduating from high school attended Villanova University and the Harvard Law School. He began his legal career in Miami, settling in the center of Little Havana, so that he could, in the words of a friend, "learn how to speak Spanish—his was pretty rusty—and develop a sense of his people."

Suarez devoted himself to serving the city's Cuban Americans and delighted especially in pro bono work, performed free of charge in the public service. One colleague who knew him remembered the time when he found Suarez in his office, surrounded by hundreds of files for his pro bono cases: "We asked him what

Veterans of the Bay of Pigs conflict stage a demonstration during the 1987 Pan American Games.

was in the boxes and he said it was his pro bono work. We almost fainted. Most young lawyers have five or ten pro bono files, this guy had five boxes of files!"

Suarez began earning a reputation as a "champion of the people." When he decided to begin a career in politics, he at first met with little luck, losing elections for the position of city commissioner in 1979 and 1981. In 1983 he challenged the candidacy of Miami's mayor Maurice A. Ferre but failed to unseat him. Despite these initial defeats, Suarez's reputation grew among his major supporters—Miami's Hispanic community. According to the *New York Times*: "Suarez in his appearances and advertising stressed a populist theme, calling himself 'the people's candidate.' "

Indeed, on learning of his victory against another Cuban-born opponent in the mayoral election of 1985, Suarez quoted the Cuban patriot José Martí: "A great man once said: '*Con los pobres de la tierra quiero yo mi suerte echar*—With the poor people of this earth I want to share my fate.' " Suarez proved true to his word, not only intervening with federal authorities on behalf of

In 1985 Xavier Suarez and his wife, Rita, leave the voting precinct after casting their ballots in the mayoral election.

the Marielitos but also aiding Miami's neglected black community.

Dade County's various groups may never form a true coalition, but Cuban-American leaders such as Xavier Suarez continually work to mend the differences between the "many Miamis." Their challenge is perhaps greatest within the city's large Spanish-speaking community, which includes people from Cuba, Puerto Rico, Mexico, the Dominican Republic, and other Latin American nations. These groups share a common language, heritage, and colonial history, but there are profound political, social, and economic differences among them—a fact that is true not just in Miami but nationwide. Hispanic Americans are not a single large body, but rather a culturally and politically diverse group. Cubans, like other Hispanic Americans, resent being lumped together with all people of Latin American descent.

One distinctive feature of Cuban-American life is Santeria, an Afro-Cuban religious cult. While most Cubans share the belief in Roman Catholicism that is central to the lives of nearly all Latin Americans, some also participate in the folk rituals of Santeria. The cult originated in Cuba's Oriente province; historians have traced it to Yoruba slaves, brought to Cuba from Africa in the 18th century. In time, Santeria was adopted by the island's colonists, whose descendants brought it to the United States. By the 1980s, Miami had about 75 stores selling Santeria paraphernalia, including potions and the Orisha, a book that details ritual practices. About 50,000 people, less than 10 percent of the area's Cuban-American population, were practitioners of Santeria. In recent years, varying forms of Santeria have begun to gain popularity among non-Cubans of Latin American descent. ✎

In 1980 Cuban immigrant children receive baptism in a Pennsylvania church.

In 1941 Carmen Miranda (front right) and Cesar Romero starred in the Hollywood extravaganza Weekend in Havana.

CUBAN-AMERICAN ACHIEVEMENTS

Cuban Americans have often been praised for their entrepreneurial talents, but their gifts extend beyond the world of business into such varied fields as the performing arts, sports, film, and literature. Dancers of Cuban descent dazzle audiences with bravura performances of such ballets as *Swan Lake* and *La Sylphide*, and Cuban-American instrumentalists lend new interpretations to the works of great classical composers. Yet the majority of Americans first heard Cuban musicians not in the concert hall but in the dance hall.

During the 1930s Don Azpiazu's Havana Casino Orchestra introduced American audiences to the sounds of maracas, bongos, congas, and timbales—traditional Caribbean instruments. A decade later, big bands from Cuba enlivened American tunes with Latin rhythms called the *son*, the *rumba*, and the *danzon*. The new beat caught the attention of top American jazz players such as Dizzy Gillespie, who learned Afro-Cuban percussion from the congo player Chano Pozo. The "Cuban sound" gained nationwide popularity and inspired Hollywood movies such as RKO's *Too Many Girls* (1940) and the Twentieth Century Fox extravaganza *Weekend*

Salsa artists Celia Cruz and Tito Puente have performed together more than 500 times.

in Havana (1941). In time, the many idioms of Latin music yielded their popularity to a fast-paced style the Cubans called *guaracha*, today known as salsa.

In America, the popularity of salsa grew with the number of Spanish-speaking immigrants who flooded the country during the 1960s and 1970s. According to one critic, "the young Puerto Ricans and Cubans in New York, New Jersey, and Miami began to take a new pride in their roots, and salsa became the musical symbol of their rediscovered identity."

The Queen of Salsa

Most aficionados of this era of Cuban music agreed that the reigning queen of salsa was Celia Cruz, a musician who began her career singing with a Havana band during the 1940s. For the next 20 years Cruz commanded a devoted following throughout Cuba, sometimes taking her act to nearby countries. In 1960—a year after Fidel Castro had assumed power—she traveled to North America to perform and seized the opportunity to seek political asylum. She told an interviewer years later, "Castro never forgave me," and explained that she had tried to return to Cuba for her father's funeral but was barred by the government from entering the country.

In America, Cruz continued to perform in the dynamic style her old admirers loved. An article in the *New York Times* described her on stage:

> . . . she leaps, dances, flaunts, flirts and teases to the gyrating beat of the salsa. She improvises playfully, trading riffs [musical phrases] with the chorus and instrumentalists. And just when she seems deeply lost in a song about a doomed love affair—microphone clutched, eyes closed, tears imminent—she looks out at the audience and tosses them an aside ("The man was a jerk anyway").

Cruz's stage theatrics and extravagant costumes—one gown trailed a 5-foot train sewn of more than 400 lace handkerchiefs—earned her fame as an entertainer. But her music, much more than mere spectacle, has earned her the respect of music critics such as Robert Palmer, who called her "an incendiary performer under just about any circumstances." In 1987 Cruz released her 53rd album, "The Winners," and also received the New York Music Award for the Best Latin Artist and her fourth nomination for the Oscars of the music industry, the Grammy awards. And after more than 40 years in the business she has no intention of slowing down. In the words of salsa percussionist Tito Puente, with whom Cruz has performed more than 500 times, "She keeps musicians on their toes."

Cuban Keyboard Artists

Although salsa vocalists such as Celia Cruz have earned a place in annals of American music, they lack the broad following enjoyed by classical musicians of Cuban descent, performers such as Horacio Gutiérrez and Jorge Bolet. In 1959, Gutiérrez made his piano debut at the age of 11 with the Havana Symphony Orchestra. Two years later, he immigrated to Miami with his parents, then moved to Los Angeles to study with Sergei Tarnowsky, who earlier taught the virtuoso Vladimir Horowitz, with whom Gutiérrez has been compared. In 1970 the young musician journeyed to Moscow to play in the prestigious Tchaikovsky Competition and won a silver medal that launched his brilliant career.

After returning home from the Soviet Union, Gutiérrez began a grueling routine of world tours, performing about 60 to 70 concerts a year. Yet his success never made him complacent. In 1987 he told an interviewer:

> You can never have enough technique, you can never have enough feeling—it's limitless. And I'm not talking about being able to play fast and loud, but being able to control what you want to play, and to express what you feel. . . . the music is greater than you are ever able to express it.

Like many top concert pianists, Horacio Gutiérrez launched his professional career by winning a medal at the Tchaikovsky Competition, held annually in Moscow.

Jorge Bolet plays on a piano that once belonged to the German composer Franz Liszt.

Since winning the Moscow competition, Gutiérrez has played and performed with the world's most renowned orchestras and won the Avery Fisher Prize, awarded to young artists of achievement. Unfortunately, professional fame has come less easily to his colleague and compatriot Jorge Bolet who, like Gutiérrez, proved himself an exceptional musician while still a child in Havana. In 1927, when Bolet was only 12, an American benefactor sent him to the United States to audition at the country's finest conservatories.

During his trip Bolet gained admission to Philadelphia's Curtis Institute of Music, where he mastered an extensive classical repertoire in only seven years of study. His exposure to the music of the 19th century left the young pianist with an affinity for the works of romantic composers such as Franz Schubert, Franz Liszt, Pyotr Tchaikovsky, and Sergey Rachmaninoff. In time, Bolet built a reputation for sensitive interpretations of their works and came to be known as "one of the great Liszt pianists of the century." Another reviewer commented that Bolet "is unique because, although first and foremost a romantic virtuoso, [he] is quite without the excesses of nineteenth-century romanticism."

Despite his many accolades—and his record of 10 performances with the New York Philharmonic in a single season—Bolet did not soar to star stature. In 1975 he told an interviewer:

> Unfortunately, I have never had the kind of overnight success that so many young pianists of today enjoy. I have arrived through a very, very slow process of constantly maturing and growing. Actually, I don't regret this. I think there is something quite lethal in quick success. I have watched dozens of young pianists receiving early success, and four or five years later they are finished. One does not hear about them again.

For a time Bolet redirected his talent toward teaching the piano rather than performing on it and found his instruction very much in demand. His new career took him to America's most esteemed conservatories, including the Indiana University School of Music and his alma mater, the Curtis Institute of Music. By the mid-1980s, however, the pianist had gained new popularity, returning to the stage and the recording studio in order to bring the masterworks he loves to a wide range of listeners.

Fernando Bujones

The personal modesty of both Gutiérrez and Bolet stand in stark contrast to the brash self-confidence of the international ballet star Fernando Bujones. In 1976 the dancer told *Dance Magazine*: "I know very well just how good I am. When I go on stage to perform, I feel secure and confident. I know what I can do, and it's a very exhilarating feeling . . . so I just let myself go. I don't think that's arrogance." Bujones derives his security, in part, from the support of his closely knit family, who immigrated from Cuba during the 1950s, settling temporarily in Miami, where Bujones was born in 1955. Shortly afterward, the clan returned home, and Bujones spent his first 10 years in Cuba. Still, he maintains, "The fact is that I am an American—born in this country. But my very early years were spent in Cuba, and that's where I started to study ballet—at the age of eight at the Alicia Alonsa School."

After learning the rudiments of ballet in Cuba, Bujones returned to Miami, where his mother—then a stage manager—arranged a private meeting with Jacques d'Amboise, a soloist in America's most respected classical dance company, the New York City Ballet. D'Amboise took the young Bujones under his wing and arranged an audition for him at the School of American Ballet in New York City. There Bujones continued the rigorous training he had begun in Cuba and developed the elegance of line and technical brilliance that now characterize his art.

As his graduation approached, Bujones prepared to enter a professional dance troupe, several of which offered him an ensemble position in their corps de ballet.

Fernando Bujones became an international ballet star at age 19.

He chose the American Ballet Theater (ABT), a repertory company specializing in productions of full-length classical ballets, such as *Coppelia, Swan Lake, Don Quixote, La Sylphide,* and *La Bayadere.* After six months in the corps, Bujones graduated to principal roles. His "aura of authority and theatrical panache" on stage earned him the praise of Antony Tudor, a British choreographer whose innovations have helped shape 20th-century dance. Tudor proved to be one of Bujones's greatest teachers.

In 1974 Bujones became the first American to win a gold medal at the International Ballet Competition in Varma, Bulgaria, the Olympics of the ballet world. He masterfully executed solo dances from *La Fille Mal Gardée, La Sylphide,* and the rhumba variation from the American ballet *Fancy Free,* thus inspiring the contest's judges to honor him not only with the first place prize, but also with a special citation for technical mastery. Bujones had achieved world fame at age 19.

His triumphant return to the United States was eclipsed, however, by headline news about the American debut of another dance star, the Russian Mikhail Baryshnikov—a defector from Leningrad's Kirov ballet. Baryshnikov soon joined Bujones's company and thereby ignited a rivalry that smoldered for 11 years, until Bujones left the company midseason in August 1985.

The dancer—who had tired of the ABT's artistic restraints—gained the freedom to perform around the world, traveling as far as Japan to appear as the guest soloist of foreign companies. In 1986 he told an interviewer, "There's so much to do. I feel like a child again."

A Sports Success

A well-known Cuban-American athlete is Tony Oliva, who began playing major-league baseball for the Minnesota Twins in 1964. Born in a province of Cuba, Oliva began his career on one of the national teams that supplied American baseball with some of its greatest Cuban players, including Vic Powers, Luis Tiant, Preston Gomez, and Mike González. In 1960 a Minnesota Twins scout spotted the 18-year-old athlete on the field and offered him a chance at a minor league tryout. Oliva, then named Pedro, traveled to the United States on his brother Tony's passport and decided to keep that first name as his own. The trip resulted not in a major league position—for which he was twice refused—but in a job playing for a Class D team in the Appalachian Rookie League.

During his first year in Appalachia, Oliva hit 10 homers and scored 81 runs, batting .410 for the season—the highest average in organized baseball that year. In 1964 his explosive hitting propelled him into the major leagues. Oliva finally won a first-string position on the Minnesota Twins and vindicated his earlier rejection by earning the Rookie of the Year award and the first of three batting titles. In the following season, Tony "O" hit a superb .321 and drove in 98 runs, powering the Twins to their 1965 pennant victory.

Oliva remained with the Twins for another 11 years, until a knee injury forced him off the field and into a coaching position in 1976. Since then he has translated his athletic talent into training know-how, instructing Twins rookies in the art of hitting, thus helping to guide the team to a World Series triumph in 1987.

Tony Oliva of the Minnesota Twins was named Rookie of the Year and helped his team win the pennant.

A Business Leader

Cuban-born Robert Goizueta assumed the joint office of chairman and chief executive of the Coca-Cola Company in 1980. Goizueta took the conglomerate's helm during a period of decline within the company, which had gradually been losing its domestic market to Pepsi-Cola—called "the imitator" by Goizueta. The new chairman insisted on a more aggressive marketing strategy and diversified Coca-Cola's holdings, acquiring Columbia Pictures for $695 million in 1982 and boosting the company's stock prices by nearly 60 percent.

Goizueta's success surprised no one who knew him well. In 1950, he arrived in America at age 18 to finish high school at the Cheshire Academy, an East Coast prep school. Some of his classmates assumed that he was spoiled because of his family background of wealth and privilege, but Goizueta proved unexpectedly industrious. Although he initially had little command of English, he attained fluency within a year—after "many sleepless nights studying the dictionary"—and graduated from Cheshire as class valedictorian. That September Goizueta entered Yale University in order to study chemical engineering. He graduated in 1954, and his Ivy League degree won him a job as a quality-control chemist at a Coca-Cola plant in Havana.

For the next 26 years Goizueta climbed Coke's corporate ladder. He worked on the island of Nassau as the head of the company's Caribbean operations and soon became second in command of the Latin American division. Goizueta again increased his responsibilities when he moved to Atlanta, Georgia—the location of Coca-Cola's corporate headquarters—and remained there, eventually assuming charge of the entire company. His bilingualism and Latin background gave him a distinct professional advantage in a company that received two-thirds of its earnings from outside the United States.

Literary Figures

The Cuban-American community has produced a number of important writers. Lydia Cabrera, consid-

Cuban-born Roberto Goizueta assumed the leadership of the Coca-Cola Company in 1981.

ered by some to be Cuba's foremost woman writer of the 20th century, is noted for her studies of Afro-Cuban folklore, beginning with *Contes negres de Cuba* (Black Stories from Cuba), published in 1936. Jose Sanchez-Boudy, a prolific author of history, folklore studies, poetry, and fiction, was born in Havana in 1928 and moved to the United States in 1961, eventually settling in North Carolina, where he became a professor of Caribbean literature. His *Poemas de silencio* (Poems of Silence, 1969) reminisces about the old days in Cuba, and his novel *Lilayando* (1971) portrays Cuban life in the United States.

The Cuban-American experience has provided material for the fiction of a younger generation of writers, including playwright and journalist Dolores Prida, author of the bilingual play *Coser y cantar* (Sewing and Singing, 1981), and Celedonio Gonzalez, whose 1971 novel *Los primos* (The Cousins) follows the lives of three young men in exile from Castro's Cuba. Roberto Fernandez, who was born in Cuba in 1951 and came to the United States with his family at the age of 10, represents the new generation of Cuban-American writers who grew up in America. His novels, written in Spanish, explore with irony and affection the lifestyles and concerns of the Cuban exile community in Miami; his major works are *La vida es un special* (Life Is on Special, 1982) and *La montana rusa* (The Roller Coaster, 1985). The Cuban-American author best known to the general reading public is Oscar Hijuelos, whose 1983 ethnic autobiography *Our House in the Last World* marked the entry of Cuban Americans into the American literary mainstream. In 1987, the *New York Times* promoted the work of Cuban-born Reinaldo Arenas, who arrived in the United States in 1980. The *Times* singled out for praise Arenas's novels *The Ill-fated Peregrinations of Fray Servando* and *Singing from the Well.* ✎

Cuban Americans in Union City, New Jersey, demonstrate against the Soviet presence in their homeland.

THE STRUGGLE FOR ACCEPTANCE

Few American ethnic groups have achieved the rapid-fire success of the Cubans. Many immigrants from the island arrived in the United States with only the clothing on their back and 5 dollars in U.S. currency, but within 25 years these exiles—the "refugee problem" of the early 1960s—climbed to positions of prominence in their new home. According to Carlos J. Arboleya, a Miami banker of Cuban descent, "[In 1983] Cuban-American developers and construction firm owners accounted for greater than 1.1 billion dollars in project development." And from 1975 to 1984 the average Hispanic family income in Dade County—where Miami is situated—increased nearly 200 percent, from $10,000 to $27,000. As Cuban Americans gained prestige and prosperity, so, too, did Miami and its environs—home to approximately 700,000 Cuban immigrants. Once a backwater, Miami became a dynamic urban center with a skyline featuring structures designed by such leading architects as Philip Johnson and I. M. Pei.

In education, too, Cubans have fared well, averaging 12.4 years of schooling in 1988. Census data collected two years later showed that 20 percent of Cuban Americans between the ages of 25 and 34 had completed at least four years of college. According to the 1990 census, Cubans were the most successful of the

A shrine for Our Lady of Charity, the patron saint of Cuba, sits amid a busy thoroughfare in Miami.

Latin American immigrant groups, differing little from the total U.S. population averages in both earnings and education. In many ways, however, the Cubans were not typical immigrants. Unlike the Mexicans and the Puerto Ricans, they came to the United States largely as political refugees rather than job seekers, and they included a far higher proportion of educated and skilled people than has been the case with the other groups.

Cuban Americans have done a good job of becoming part of America without losing their distinctive ethnic identity. Gloria Estefan, the enormously successful Miami singer, may stand as a symbol of Cuban-American assimilation into the U.S. mainstream. Estefan was born in Havana, Cuba, in 1958; the following year her family fled to the United States after Castro's takeover. Estefan began performing traditional Cuban music for parties and dances in the Cuban community in Miami, but by the 1980s her band had begun to release pop hits that transcended the "Latin music" category, and soon Estefan was recognized as a popular music star. She has continued to record Latin music in Spanish while at the same time producing a string of pop hits in English—an example of an immigrant who has found a way to express her ethnic heritage without being limited by it.

Despite the growing acceptance of Cuban Americans, many people both outside and within the Cuban-American community are uncertain about the future of Cubans in the United States. Do they still think of themselves as exiles, or are they committed to life in America? Even many of the Cuban Americans, especially the older generation, cannot answer. But after several decades in the United States, some have grown resigned to the loss of "old Cuba." Others, however, are determined to recreate the Havana of their youth in south Florida.

Those Cuban Americans born in the United States often struggle to forge a new identity as both Cubans and Americans. But no matter how assimilated they

become, Cuban Americans maintain their fierce pride in their heritage and realize that their community judges them foremost on their devotion to their native land.

By the 1980s, most Cuban Americans had struck a balance between nostalgia for their homeland and acceptance of their indefinite state of exile. Yet even as they forged a new identity in the United States, Cuban Americans kept alive the dream of a free Cuba. ✎

In 1983 the José Fajardo Orchestra celebrated the birthday of José Martí in Union City, New Jersey.

Further Reading

Boswell, Thomas D. *The Cuban-American Experience: Culture, Images and Perspectives*. Totowa, N.J.: Rowman and Allanheld, 1984.

Chavez, Linda. *Out of the Barrio: Toward a New Politics of Hispanic Assimilation*. New York: Basic Books, 1991.

Didion, Joan. *Miami*. New York: Simon & Schuster, 1987.

Fagen, Richard R. *Cubans in Exile: Disaffection and the Revolution*. Palo Alto, Cal.: Stanford University Press, 1968.

Fairbairns, Douglas. *Street B*. New York: Delacorte, 1977.

Franqui, Carlos. *Family Portrait with Fidel: A Memoir*. New York: Vintage, 1985.

Garver, Susan and Paula McGuire. *Coming to America: From Mexico, Cuba, and Puerto Rico*. New York: Delacorte, 1981.

Grenquist, Barbara. *Cubans*. New York: Franklin Watts, 1991.

Mendoza, Tony. *Stories*. New York: Atlantic Monthly Press, 1987.

Perez, Gustavo. *Life on the Hyphen: The Cuban-American Way*. Austin: University of Texas Press, 1994.

Rieff, David. *The Exile: Cuban in the Heart of Miami*. New York: Simon & Schuster, 1993.

——————. *Going to Miami*. Boston: Little, Brown, 1987.

Suchlicki, Jaime. *Cuba: From Columbus to Castro*. New York: Scribners, 1974.

Thomas, Hugh. *The Cuban Revolution*. New York: Harper & Row, 1977.

INDEX

PICTURE CREDITS

RENEE GERNAND graduated with honors from the University of Virginia. A writer and editor, she has written book reviews for the *New York Times*. She lives in New York City.

SANDRA STOTSKY is director of the Institute on Writing, Reading, and Civic Education at the Harvard Graduate School of Education as well as a research associate there. She is also editor of *Research in the Teaching of English,* a journal sponsored by the National Council of Teachers of English.

Dr. Stotsky holds a bachelor of arts degree with distinction from the University of Michigan and a doctorate in education from the Harvard Graduate School of Education. She has taught on the elementary and high school levels and at Northeastern University, Curry College, and Harvard. Her work in education has ranged from serving on academic advisory boards to developing elementary and secondary curricula as a consultant to the Polish Ministry of Education. She has written numerous scholarly articles, curricular materials, encyclopedia entries, and reviews and is the author or coauthor of three books on education.

REBECCA STEFOFF is a writer and editor who has published more than 50 nonfiction books for young adults. Many of her books deal with geography, environmental issues, and exploration, including the three-volume set *Extraordinary Explorers*. She has worked with Ronald Takaki in adapting *Strangers from a Distant Shore* into a 15-volume Chelsea House series, the ASIAN AMERICAN EXPERIENCE. Stefoff studied English at the University of Pennsylvania, where she taught for three years. She lives in Portland, Oregon.

REED UEDA is associate professor of history at Tufts University. He graduated summa cum laude with a bachelor of arts degree from UCLA, received master of arts degrees from both the University of Chicago and Harvard University, and received a doctorate in history from Harvard.

Dr. Ueda was research editor of the *Harvard Encyclopedia of American Ethnic Groups* and has served on the board of editors for *American Quarterly, Harvard Educational Review, Journal of Interdisciplinary History,* and *University of Chicago School Review*. He is the author of several books on ethnic studies, including *Postwar Immigrant America: A Social History, Ethnic Groups in History Textbooks,* and *Immigration*.

DANIEL PATRICK MOYNIHAN is the senior United States senator from New York. He is also the only person in American history to serve in the cabinets or subcabinets of four successive presidents—Kennedy, Johnson, Nixon, and Ford. Formerly a professor of government at Harvard University, he has written and edited many books, including *Beyond the Melting Pot, Ethnicity: Theory and Experience* (both with Nathan Glazer), *Loyalties,* and *Family and Nation.*